THERAPY IN SESSIONS

What you pretend not to know

*The **POWER** of your inner voice*

Joanne Suarez
Secrets on how to be happy daily

Joanne Suarez "Diosa"

With a clear but simple mission of helping and inspiring others, today Joanne Suarez is not only the author of this great book but an amazing Entrepreneur. She is a proud single mother of two, certified life coach, certified medical assistant, dance instructor, fitness model, artist, notary public, and a proud motivational speaker that is loved and known for making a memorable impact in her life, as well as in others.

Her unique approach combined with exceptional knowledge and guidance, outgoing personality, strength, courage, contagious laugh, and enthusiasm makes her a perfect candidate to inspire on how you can make a difference in life.

Through her own experiences and unknown battles forced to fight, she overcame the war and found healing by providing the right tools and knowledge to others. Diosa has helped people unleash their potential and believe in themselves, paving the way towards both personal and professional success fulfilled with Peace and Love.

Table of Contents

.

WHAT ARE YOU PRETENDING NOT TO KNOW?

Before you read ahead, let us practice this exercise. I want you to look at the dotted pattern below. Grab a pencil or something to write with and make 9 dots just as the ones you see. The task is to connect all 9 dots using only 4 straight lines without ever picking up the pencil or retracing any of the lines.

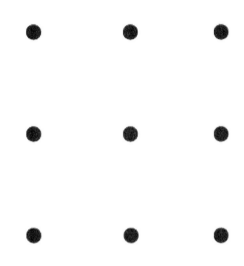

If you got it, you are one step closer to achieving your goals, or you are possibly already there striving for more. If you feel like it is not possible, or you are having trouble making it happen. I ask you, what are you pretending not to know? Pretending not to know is a habit. It is known as an emotional defense mechanism. You must finally learn that life is lived during the pauses or breaks when we make time to reflect and genuinely appreciate the moment.

The biggest difference is that pretending means you know something but act as if you don't. You can pretend not to know both positive and negative things. This I know for a fact. People use this method to find out just how much you know or don't know. I have had this experience repeatedly. Society is always searching for someone they can control. After people hear me speak, they realize that I am not some dumb ass woman hoping to get accepted by them and/or their peers. Humans are always testing you. If they find any area of weakness you can bet that they will attempt to exploit you into some sort of submissive behavior towards their advantage. As a wise human being, my conclusion is that I no longer give a damn. No one wants another person to be equal to them. The lesser is always a welcomed sight. If you play the dumb guy you will notice how many people will flock to your presence.

However, the trick is accepting that you do not need approval from anyone to be you. You do not need a bigger crowd to feel important. What you need to do is realize that what you pretend not to know is getting in the way of all that is possible for you. We often leave things inconclusive or in indecision. Waiting and waiting for the answer to come or for it to go away. We pretend not to see the "RED FLAGS" that tell us to not go ahead with something. We pretend that we are not hurt to not show up angry.

We pretend that we are happy. We pretend that everything is ok. We pretend to not know things or notice things. We pretend that we are victims when we clearly know we are responsible. I could go on and on over everything that we tend to pretend. But let's be honest, is it serving you or anyone? Avoiding what is and not accepting what holds us hostage. Not making decisions is a cloud hanging over your shoulder tiring you out to exhaustion. We are always at choice and noticing what you are pretending not to know could be the beginning of a new life.

Might sound silly but try it. See what happens. What would your life be like if you took risks more often and trusted yourself that you can figure things out along the way? What if you stopped ignoring the "RED FLAGS"? You would no longer sabotage yourself in that way. What if you just allowed yourself to experience sadness and hurt? There would be one less angry person in this world. What if you would start making decisions? You would have peace of mind and everything would fall in place. You can pretend with others but ultimately you must live with you. You are the one who lives with all this pretending.

I am challenging you. Write down all the things that you have been pretending not to know. Then really be with it. How has this been serving you and how has it been holding you back? More importantly, who is paying the prices? Why do people pretend to know things? Why does confidence so often scale with ignorance? I believe we are biased to preserve our sense of rightness. I am especially interested in what's called "the illusion of explanatory depth." This is how cognitive scientists refer to our tendency to overestimate our understanding of how the world works. We do this because of our reliance on other minds. The decisions we make, the attitudes we form, the judgments we make, depend very much on what other people are thinking. If the people around us are wrong about something, there is a good chance we will be too.

Proximity to truth compounds in the same way. I really do believe that our attitudes are shaped much more by our social groups than they are by facts on the ground. We are not great reasoners. Most people don't like to think at all. Or like to think as little as possible. And by most, I mean roughly seventy percent of the population. Even the rest seem to devote a lot of their resources to justifying beliefs that they want to hold, as opposed to forming credible beliefs based only on facts. Think about if you were to complete a fact that contradicted the opinions of the majority of those in your group, you pay a price for that. If I said I voted for Trump, most of my friends would think I am crazy. They probably would not want to talk to me. That is how social pressure influences our logical commitments, and it often does it in invisible ways.

However, this is another way of saying that we live in a community of knowledge. That's right! I believe every thought we have depends on thoughts that other people are having. When I cross the street, my actions depend on the thoughts that are going through the mind of the driver's head. If I get on the bus, the success of my attempt to make it depends on the thoughts that are going on in the bus driver's head. When I express an attitude about immigration, what am I really doing? What do I really know about immigration? I live in an extremely limited universe, so I must depend on the beliefs and knowledge of other people. I know what I have read. I know what I have heard from experts. But I do not have any direct experience on the immigration problem. I have not visited the border or studied it myself. In that sense, the decisions we make, the attitudes we form and the judgments we make, depend very much on what other people are thinking.

There are some obvious dangers here, right? One danger is that if I think I understand because the people around me think they understand. At this point, the people around me all think they understand because the people around them all think they understand. Then it turns out we can all have this strong sense of understanding even though no one really has any idea what they are talking about. I am trying to think about all of this in terms of our political circumstances. Most of us do not understand as much as we think, yet we are all sure as cocks about a range of issues. When we are arguing about politics, what are we really arguing about? Is it about getting it right or is it about preserving our sense of rightness?

I am not sure there is a large distinction between wanting to get it right and wanting to preserve our sense of rightness. In the political domain, like most domains in which we don't just hear or see what's true, we rely on social consciousness. The arguments are about trying to convince others while we are trying to convince ourselves. Getting it right essentially means we are convinced and of course, we are biased to preserve our sense of rightness, but we must be. If we weren't, we would be starting again each time we approached an issue, and our previous arguments would be for naught.

Nevertheless, people differ on this. Everyone has a compulsion to be right. Meaning that they want the people around them to think they are right. This is easily achieved by mouthing the things that the people around you say. People who are more capable tend to be better at finding ways to interpret new facts. Some people do try to rise above the crowd to verify claims independently. To give fair hearing to others claims and to follow the data where it leads. In fact, many people are trained to do that. Scientists, judges, investigators, physicians, etc. That does not mean they always do (and they don't always), just that they're supposed to try. And yet at times pretend not to know.

Do you have any thoughts in terms of practical solutions to this? How can we cultivate more self-awareness and less biased reasoning? How can we seek out wiser communities of knowledge? People who are more reflective are less susceptible to the illusion. There are some simple questions you can use to measure reflectivity. They tend to have this form: How many animals of each kind did Moses load onto the ark? Most people say two, but more reflective people say zero. (It was Noah, not Moses who built the ark). The trick is to not only conclude but to verify that conclusion. You just need one person to say, "Are you sure?" And for everyone else to care about the justification. There is no reason for the world not to adopt these kinds of norms. The problem of course is that there is a strong compulsion to make people feel good by telling them what they want to hear, and for everyone to agree. That is largely what gives us a sense of identity.

I was doing some research on whether one way to open discipline is to try to change the nature of conversation from a focus on what people value to one about actual consequence. When you talk about actual consequences, you are forced into the weeds of what is happening. Which is a diversion from our normal focus on our feelings and what's going on in our heads. Most people go through life with some level of pretending. Our earliest childhood games involved pretending. Those games helped us learn to interact with each other and the world. Childhood pretending has many positive effects.

Adult pretending tends to have a negative impact. It can diminish your self-esteem and destroy your credibility. You know from your own experiences that it causes problems when you pretend things are different than they are. It is likely that you have worked for a person who pretended not to know things. Looked the other way when problems

13

occurred or acted in a way that didn't align with what you knew was true. It probably made it challenging to maintain a healthy level of respect for that person. Look at the power of denial and how that denial can help you be effective.

Here, we will explore how your own pretending, or the pretending of your followers can limit effectiveness. For the purposes of leadership, pretending is acting as if something exists, or does not exist, when you know deep in your core that the opposite is true. How does pretending differ from denial? The biggest difference is that pretending means you know something but act as if you don't. Pretending not to know has a few theories. There are differences, for example, there are differences between people who say they do not care versus people who don't care. Have you ever met anyone that just seemed to have a low threshold for nonsense?

They rarely allow anything or anyone to bother them. There is a difference between people who pretend they don't care versus people who don't care. That is knowing their self-worth. We have all had that moment where we have made the declaration of not caring anymore. Perhaps it's that split second when you think someone is waving at you. Only to realize that you do not know them, and they are greeting the person behind you. You feel a little embarrassed but shrug, (whatever I don't care). Maybe it was that date that left your message unread that ghosted you and got you to get out of bed for nothing. Yet you feel a little wounded but throw your hands up saying, (I didn't care anyway). The truth is, that it is ok to feel hurt, upset, or whatever uncomfortable emotions emerge when someone has wronged you. The key is not to dwell on these emotions or allow them to foster resentment within your being.

- ❖ The person who pretends they don't care is going to ignore their hurt feelings and vulnerability.

- ❖ The person who does not care is going to acknowledge and embrace their feelings.

- ❖ The person who pretends they don't care is going to drag your name and business through the streets.

- ❖ The person who doesn't care is not going to spend hours gossiping over you.

- ❖ The person who pretends they don't care is going to answer the phone call because they want to hear the explanation.

- ❖ The person who doesn't care isn't going to answer the call- they may call back if it's convenient for them.

- ❖ The person who pretends they don't care is going to nag, complain, and whine.

- ❖ The person who doesn't care is going to let their actions speak for themselves by distancing themselves from you.

- ❖ The person who pretends they don't care is going to make excuses for unwanted behavior.

- ❖ The person that doesn't care believes that we are all accountable for our own behavior.

- ❖ The person who pretends they don't care is going to teach you how you can do better.

- ❖ The person who doesn't care is continually working on self-improvement and isn't going to spend all their time trying to fix you.

- ❖ The person who pretends they do not care is going to be bitter and resentful.

- ❖ The person who does not care is going to be thankful that they saw your true colors.

- ❖ The person who pretends they don't care is going to negotiate with you.

- ❖ The person who doesn't care adapts a zero-tolerance mentality to disrespect.

- ❖ The person who pretends they don't care is going to secretly stalk you on social media.

- ❖ The person who doesn't care is going to block you on social media if you disregard their boundaries.

If you are someone that finds yourself struggling with closure, or having people continually cross your boundaries, some of these may seem even a little heartless to you. Not actually caring has nothing to do with being cruel or unsympathetic towards people. It has everything to do with stating your boundaries, sticking to them, and loving yourself enough to walk away if necessary. It does not happen overnight. It does not mean that you don't feel hurt, betrayal, or loss. What it does mean is that despite your feelings, you know your self-worth and what you deserve. Feelings are temporary, you can work on them. But dignity is priceless. Next time someone wrongs you ask yourself, am I pretending that I do not care? Or am I going to work on not caring?

I will tell you the importance of letting yourself be yourself. I would like to ask you; how do you feel about the way you appear within the context of your life? Are you truly yourself? Do you feel that you can be you no matter the situation you are in? If you regularly feel that you cannot just relax and be yourself, you are probably sick and tired of it or life itself. There is a good chance that you put on different masks so habitually that you do not even notice when you are doing it. Maybe you have done it your whole life. I have been writing lately about exhaustion and conserving a positive energy. It is a huge drain on your mind, body and soul to frequently pretend to be, or feel like you need to be, someone else.

Similarly, it's very draining to regularly act like you feel one way when you really feel another, but don't allow yourself (or don't feel it's safe) to express your truth. I can assure you that dropping the habitual masks you put on to please and impress others will be crucial to transforming and healing your life. Faking your way through life is believing that if you let people know the real you, they will not like you. Maybe it seems that nothing you ever do is ever enough. The tapes that play in your head say that if people really knew what was going on inside of you, they would lose respect for you.

Maybe you will keep trying to pretend to make others happy. You will be exhausted physically, mentally, and spiritually. While you play those roles juggling those masks that you wear while hiding in pain. The pressure increases to keep pretending you have it all together. Let us consider more the cost of our souls and the loss of ourselves when we do this. Take it from me, I would have never discovered my true identity, unless I began identifying and laying down my masks. Like everything in life, all we do is go through a process.

Here is my recommendation. Below are some questions that I suggest you consider helping you drop your own masks. I recommend you explore your answers in writing. Maybe even address a question a day to let your truth emerge deeply over a period of time.

Think about all the times in your life when you felt you had to be ok when you could not be honest with how you really felt. When you chose to pretend to be someone you were not. What is the cause of that?

+ If I were to ask you to describe yourself, could you talk about your strengths and weaknesses with confidence? (In other words, do you know who you really are?)

+ Do you always act the same regardless of the situation you are in?

+ When you are around others, do you ever feel strained and uncomfortable and find it hard to relax?

+ Has anyone ever told you that they thought you were one way, but then when they got to know you better, realized you were another way?

+ Has anyone ever commented on how you act differently around various people?

+ Do you ever act like you do not care what others think but deep down it really hurts when others judge or reject you?

+ Do you ever pretend to like someone you really do not?

What might some of your masks be? The, "I've got it all together" mask? The, "I'm a victim mask"? Think about different situations in your life's work, school, home, with friends, with family, etc... What mask might emerge during those times?

There are obviously times when it is adaptive to protect your true self or your feelings and thoughts. Some people and situations are not safe and it's wise to hold back. With that being said, if you identify yourself as frequently donning masks in "unsafe" situations (where you fear criticism, belittling, anger, etc.), it may be worth looking at how to reduce your exposure to these people and situations. As you become more aware of the circumstances in which you put on a certain mask, do not be frustrated if you can't change your behavior right away.

You've likely been doing this for years, maybe even your entire life. Be patient and gentle with yourself. As I always tell people, the first step in change is simply to watch out and notice when you engage in a behavior that you want to change. Notice what event or person triggered the donning of a mask. How did it feel when you were wearing it? How did you feel afterwards? Did it achieve anything? Was there a negative result? What would you like to do differently the next time you're in that situation to be more authentic?

Awareness is everything. Do not put pressure on yourself to change overnight and be compassionate with yourself. Trust that if you set the goal of being more real via the dropping of your habitual masks, you will be able to do this with time. It will feel so damn good! All you must do is trust the process. Why do we pretend not to know, is a question with an easier answer than what we imagine? What we want to do is stop pretending and start living?

"Remembering you are going to die is the best way I know to avoid the trap of thinking you have something to lose. You are already naked. There is no reason not to follow your heart."

~Steve Jobs

Do you like your job? Do you love your partner? Are you happy? You may answer yes to these questions, but is that what you believe deep down? Most of us go through life pretending rather than living. We find it easier to tell ourselves that we feel good about something or someone than to admit we do not. After all, contentment does not require action. By convincing ourselves we are happy when we are not, we avoid the difficult decisions that would be necessary to change our current situation. If we pretend everything is fine, there is no need to quit that job we hate. We do not have to deal with all the risks, fears, and potential disapproval we might face from friends, loved ones, and family if we leave it behind.

We do not have to tell our partner that we are not in love with him or her anymore. Or that we are not happy in our relationship. We do not have to swallow our pride and ask for help when we need it because, hey, everything is simply fine right?! We can simply smile and keep pretending. We spend so much time trying to conform to society and the expectation of those around us that we lose the ability to listen to our hearts. Is it necessary to ask ourselves if we like our job or still love our spouse or partner? Do we really have to ask ourselves whether we are happy? The truth is something inside of us already knows the answer. Often, the answer lies in the fact that we must ask the question in the first place. When we are genuinely happy, we know. And when we are not, we know that too.

It does not take much courage to go through life pretending everything is all right. Exposing our true selves, fully embracing our deepest desires and facing our fears require a tremendous amount.

In all honesty, I spent many years of my life pretending. I told myself that I was happy with my life, my job. Despite knowing from the very first day that it was not the right fit for me. Knowing that I hated my boss talking down to me and having to tolerate it because she is the boss. I pretended to agree with everyone around me to avoid the risk of losing my job, rejection, and disapproval. In a way, I have even pretended to be shy when I am a natural extrovert, certainly. At the same time, acting shy was very convenient for me. At many times, it was a means to stay quiet, avoid risks, and maintain the illusion that I was better than I really was. After spending so much time hiding my true self, I finally reached a point where I had had enough of it. Enough of being fake, enough of superficial relationships, enough of trying to be liked and seeking the approval of others. Enough!

It was then that I made up my mind: I would stop pretending. I did not want to have fake relationships where people liked me for something I'm not because I was too scared to show them the real me. I didn't want to play it safe during a date for fear of failing to give the correct answer or saying the wrong thing and ruining everything. I was always trying to be the person they wanted me to be just because I wanted to be loved and thought that was a way of getting what I wanted. We all want to be loved. But if we are on a date with someone who is hyper-analyzing every little thing we do, waiting for an opportunity to reject us, how could they possibly be the right match? Even if that strategy works, aren't we running the risk of ending up in an uninspired relationship with the wrong person by pretending to be someone we aren't?

It's easier to pretend than to be truly honest with ourselves, but what's the point? It comes with a steep price. If I pretend my current job is satisfying, what are the chances that I will make the necessary changes to create a fulfilling career that will bring meaning to my life? If I pretend to be happy in a relationship when my true feelings clearly say something else, how can I improve my relationship? If I'm constantly trying to be someone I am not, how can I create meaningful relationships with people who would have loved me if only I had given them a chance to know who I really am? I wanted my relationships with others to be meaningful, profound, and emotionally rewarding.

I did not want to constantly analyze every word that crosses my mind and handpick only those that will earn me the approval of the person I'm speaking to. I wanted to be able to say that I hated something even when everyone around me loved it. As an Afro Cuban American woman living in the United States, I wanted to be able to admit that I have no interest in the political world even when everybody expected me to. I wanted to be able to say that although I love wine and cheese, I know nothing about wine and can barely eat cheese. I wanted to freely admit that I could not remember much about this person standing before me. When asked about my hobbies, I wanted to say with excitement that I love smoking marijuana rather than murmuring about others. I like watching movies and listening to music for the other parts when I'm not working on my many passions.

Oh, but these days, I am being honest. Showing the real me and saying what is true for me. I'm an entrepreneur, therefore I'm multitalented. I recently had a client who I was working on a new project with that required me to navigate between spreadsheets. I told them that I was not good at using Excel due to my lack of experience with it. In the past, I would've hidden the fact that I did not know and felt bad about it for days or even weeks. I blamed myself for not being good enough. During parties, I have no shame admitting that I hated all my previous jobs in the medical field and couldn't wait to quit because I always had dumbass bosses. In the past, I would have pretended I liked it just to fit in with everyone else. I've openly shared my passion with people I've just met, discussed the business I'm currently working on, and even talked about how I envision my future. In the past, I would have remained quiet. And yes, I have unapologetically stated the fact that I hate talking about politics.

I've been saying these things for a while, so it isn't exactly a new accomplishment for me. What is new is how I feel about saying and doing these things. I once felt guilt and shame over it, but those feelings have dissipated. At some point, I stopped feeling bad for not enjoying a Presidential conversation about politics. I stopped apologizing for not enjoying my job. I stopped blaming myself for not knowing how to use Excel. That was even more freeing than speaking my mind and staying true to myself. In other words, I went from clarifying and explaining my honest statements to saying the truth as is. Without all the unnecessary comments that I would usually add to it. I stopped apologizing for being me and stopped feeling bad about myself because of things that cannot be changed.

Pretending is costly although it is not money we give away. But rather peace of mind and happiness. Fortunately, we always have a choice. We can keep pretending everything is okay, refuse to take any risks. We can settle for an okay relationship, a mediocre job. Or we can decide to accept ourselves as we truly are, embrace our fear and discomfort, and give ourselves a chance to create a meaningful relationship both with ourselves and others outside of our comfort zone. It might be time for you to stop pretending and start being truly honest with yourself. Otherwise, you could miss a chance to find a career that leaves you excited to wake up every morning and meet people who love you for who you are. Not for who you pretend to be.

~ "One can pretend many things, including being intelligent. What cannot be pretended is happiness."

~"When you've eliminated the impossible, whatever remains, however improbable, must be the truth!"

How to apply ourselves instead of pretending

Simply express your reality. As leaders, we have difficulties facing the reality of our insecurities and sometimes we pretend they are not there so no one has to know. The truth is that who you are is always within you. We must find our strength and move forward into our reality with the parts of ourselves we love. And embody it with everything we do. There are too many of us not living our reality because we are living pretended lives. You must live your greatness because when you see great talent and capabilities in others, you may feel that you are lacking something important in yourself. Remember that the greatness you see in them is greatness you appreciate in yourself. When we are inspired by another it is because we recognize greatness within ourselves.

Let us start by mastering your imperfections. It is totally ok to be imperfect. As leaders, owning our imperfections means owning our REAL self. Pretending will never help us recognize the ways in which we are dishonest with ourselves and with others, but perfection is not the journey. Our destination is authenticity. You must lead from your sources. Leading from your source challenges you to find your dreams, intelligence, wisdom, knowledge, and creativity. Leading from your source takes courage. Living without pretending takes strength. Most people fail in life not because they think BIG but because they feel small. When we pretend to be or feel what we are not, we steal the gratification of who we really are from ourselves. Learn to lead from within, when we accept all of who we are, we are realizing all we can become.

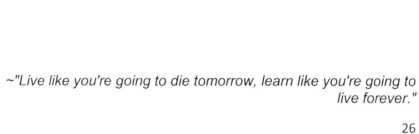

~"Live like you're going to die tomorrow, learn like you're going to live forever."

What too much pretending can do

It worries me, it really worries me. We go about our daily routines with a heavy load in our minds. It might have to do with losing weight, getting older, being lonely, family dilemmas, stagnant career progression, debt problems or any one of a multitude of troubles that life lands in our (deal with this challenge) inbox.

Yet, despite all this stuff that exists below the surface, when someone says, how are you? We are most likely to say, "I'm fine!" I get that it would be odd if we went around complaining and wallowing in self-pity all day long. Who would want to be around that? But there is going to be a downside to all this suppression, denial, and other defense mechanisms that we all employ to help us cope with our daily lots. We do our best to avoid dealing with the discomfort that is a natural part of being human. We use avoidant coping to deal with challenges in life. Long term denial can lead to self-sabotage and an inability to know what is real and what is fabricated. We justify all sorts of things to ourselves to live a life as free of internal conflict as possible.

Sure, we can try to dismiss our thoughts and be more aware when we are using cognitive distortions such as catastrophic negativity, personalizing, or black and white thinking to minimize the emotional impact of too much pretending. But I have witnessed, repeatedly, people trying too hard to explain away life challenges that cannot effectively be explained away. The typical symptoms of too much pretending is inadvertently encouraged in school. Being two faced and appeasing in the company you are with is what many kids do to be popular. (Fit in, don't be different and don't be yourself).

These are messages that modern school dynamics unwittingly teach. Schools are like acting academies. You learn to do what you must. To not be bullied, not stand out, and to be popular. It's just NOT IN to tell others you don't like something that goes against the agreement and so the conditioning begins. Learn to express yourself and talk about your feelings. When someone asks how you are, you do not need to give them your life story but if you aren't "fine" say so. If the person doesn't really want to know the answer, they shouldn't ask you. Accept that being human means experiencing hurt, self-doubt and sometimes sadness. Being happy and thrilled are also part of being human. We should embrace both equally.

~"Don't get exhausted trying to play the healer in every relationship. I know you see the potential in some people, but sometimes they do not see what you see. It is not your fault. It is not your job to help someone grow if they do not want to. It is about building together and expanding equally. It is about improving each other and balancing each other. Do not drain yourself trying to improve people. You deserve so much more. Don't settle"

Who are your real friends?

If all you had to offer was friendship, who would still be around? I came to notice that people pretend well when their souls are for sale. Sometimes it is the people that you love the most that mainly want to see you fail. That is real. Just because they ride with you, doesn't mean they ride for you. And that's a fact!

Loyalty should not depend on your presence; it is more about how they act behind your back. Who can you trust? Some of us are fighting for people that would not throw a punch for us, yet these are the ones we call true friends and family. You know, the ones that care so much about your struggles yet are so silent when you win. The ones that bring gossip to you about yourself but your name they never defend. As time goes, pay attention, everyone in your circle might not be in your corner. Support doesn't always come from familiar faces. Sometimes God places a stranger in your life to take you to higher places. Don't be surprised if your growth makes your circle smaller, sometimes to add to your life you must subtract. I have learned this the hard way being that I was never really that good at math. Understand that is not the size of your circle that matters. It is the loyalty that is in it.

Does your circle have that type of commitment? Are they happy for you when you win it? Real friends do not hate on each other, they push each other to go get it. Do you have those types of friendships in your life? Viruses are very contagious. I will promise you this, whoever you consistently surround your life around will surely persuade it. Wake up!!! Not everyone's prayers for you is to make it. Do they really love you or do they just fake it? Do they really have love for you, or do they just use you? To some, you are just an opportunity. That's how these fake friends will do you. They come into your life just to take what they need, and when they can no longer benefit from your life, well, that's when their loyalty leaves.

If all you had to offer was friendship, who would you still be able to call your friend? Take the time to let them know you appreciate them!

~ "An honest enemy is better than a false friend. When in doubt, pay more attention to what people do and less to what they say. Actions don't just speak louder than words, they're harder to fake."

Raise your kids

Word of advice:

Speak greatness into your child's life every chance you get. Never stop planting seeds of love in your child's life. Too many kids grow up not believing in themselves because their parents never believed in them. Support their dreams and expand their vision, help them reach their goals. Help them win in life. You should always be the one they run to, not run from, despite the age!

You should be the one that builds them up not break them down. Make sure you got their life, not control it. Do not limit their life because of your limitations. What you could not do has nothing to do with what they can do. Teach them to think bigger. Teach them to rise above. Understand, it is you that sets the tone for their life. Be someone they can look up to. What you instill in them will grow in them. Be someone they can really depend on. Don't forget you only get to raise your child once. So, try your best to be your best because they deserve it.

As a parent of younger kids, you read these articles and feel paralyzed, overwhelmed with fear and mixed messages. What exactly is the right thing to do? Where am I going wrong? Should I give up and start a savings account for my child's future therapy sessions?

The part that scares me the most is that we are so overwhelmed by the judgment in modern parenting that it feels safer (and by far easier) to do nothing. We turn on the TV and hide in technology Never, Never Land.

You should know something...
Change starts with one parent and one child at a time. You have a beautiful window of opportunity to build the foundation that your child desperately needs but also craves. The foundation for things like generosity, responsibility, appreciation, warmth, kindness, helpfulness, and hard-work ethic all starts during the early years. Here is the hard part. It starts with us, the parents. Kids cannot even think at the maturity level needed to break a behavior cycle, let alone do anything about it. As parents, it must start with us. The foundation for well-adjusted kids always starts with us.

Here are simple ways that help raise well-adjusted kids. Let us get back to basics, shall we?

- Boundaries

  No brainer, right? But it is hard to set boundaries for kids and stick to them. This is especially true when kids push back, scream endlessly, or threaten things like, "I hate you." Remember that when kids act this way, they are meeting their own needs in the only way they know how. Depending on the boundary, it can take a long time before a child lovingly accepts a parent's boundary. When kids start to push back or scream less, this is your child moving towards acceptance of the boundary. If your boundary is like a wall (and not a door that confusingly swings open from time to time) your child will bounce and eventually work to meet his or her need in an alternative way. The world is a very chaotic place. Boundaries help your child, not only feel grounded, but thrive. Check yourself and think about what your real boundaries are. Then remember, they are brick walls, not doors.

- Routines

  There is so much of childhood that is new and challenging for kids. Learning self-control and empathy. Learning how to be a friend and interact with others. These are all noticeably BIG things for kids. Using something as simple as printable routine flashcards can help kids feel grounded and relaxed. In fact, knowing what to expect at mealtimes, mornings and bedtimes can bring a sense of relief to even the most carefree child. Do you have a strong-willed child? Even better. Routines allow kids to feel a sense of control, something that is particularly important to a strong-willed child.

- Empathy

  What do kids really need to be happy and successful? The answer surprises most: Empathy. It is the trait that allows us to walk in another person's shoes. New research shows that empathy plays a major role in predicting kids' happiness and success. Though kids are hardwired to care, they are not born empathetic, just like they are not born knowing how to order a latte at Starbucks (wink). It is a learned behavior. "Empathy promotes kindness, prosocial behaviors, and moral courage, and it is an effective antidote to bullying, aggression, prejudice and racism." Empathy promotes essential ingredients for leadership success and excellent performance.

- Hugs

  Some of you are probably thinking "a hug, really?" Well, there's a saying: "We need four hugs a day for

survival. We need eight hugs a day for maintenance. We need twelve hugs a day for growth."
Hugging triggers the release of oxytocin, also known as the love hormone. This feel good hormone has many important effects on our bodies. One of them is growth stimulation. (True story) Studies show that hugging can instantly boost the level of oxytocin. When oxytocin is increased, several growth hormones, such as insulin-like growth factor-I (IGF-1) and nerve growth factor (NGF), are increased as well. The nurturing touch of a hug can enhance a child's growth.

- Being playful parents

Children do not say, I had a hard day, can we talk? They say, will you play with me? We do not reserve much room in our lives for fun and games anymore. Our days are filled with stress, obligations, and hard work, and without realizing it, we are more disconnected from our kids than ever. Play is the work of the child and to connect with our kids, we must play with our kids. Taking the time to put down our phones and realize that our kids need us to play. It sounds silly, but all the mindless post and stories on Instagram and Facebook and random tasty recipes will still be there years later, our children will not. We all grow up but leave some space for that kid we must keep inside us for life.

- Outdoor time

Movement through active free play, especially outside, improves everything from creativity to academic success to emotional stability. Kids who do not get to do this can have so many issues. From problems with emotional regulation for example. They cry at the drop of a hat to trouble holding a pencil, to touching other kids using too much force or to just a look of a family member they do not see often. Outdoor time is extremely important!

- Chores

  Even though it is more difficult at the time to persist in having children do chores, kids benefit from the experience. Research indicates that those children who have a set of chores have higher self-esteem, are more responsible, and are better able to deal with frustration and delay gratification. All of which contribute to greater success in school. Furthermore, research shows that involving children in household tasks at an early age can have a positive impact later in life. In fact, the best predictor of young adult's success in their mid-20 was that they participated in household tasks when they were three or four.

- More screen-time limits

  For the brain's neural networks to develop normally during the critical period, a child needs specific stimuli from the outside environment. These are rules that have evolved over centuries of human evolution, but not surprisingly these essential stimuli are not found on today's tablet screens. When a young child spends too much time in front of a screen, iPad, phone, or any of those types of gadgets and not enough getting required stimuli from the real world, their development becomes stunted.

- Experiences, not things

Children require less things and far more meaningful experiences. When they grow up, it is not the stuff in their life they will remember, it is that time you spent with them practicing for their big game or music recital. Or that sandcastle you both built at that the wave knocked over at the beach. The best life experiences cost little to nothing. A picnic in the park, blowing bubbles in the backyard, making chalk drawings on the sidewalk, or tossing a football around. They all have one thing in common. You do them together! What kids really want in life is quality time spent with their parents. Get it.

- Slow moving days

   I encourage parents to take some time to just watch their children. Whether they are playing, doing homework, or eating a snack. Take a moment to drink them in. Remember and remind yourself how remarkable your children are. That pause alone, even if momentary, can drive a shift in the pace.

- Books read to them

   One of the most important things parents can do, beyond keeping kids healthy and safe is to read with them. That means starting when they are newborns and not even able to talk, continuing well beyond the years that they can read by themselves. Study after study shows that early reading with children helps them learn to speak, interact, bond with parents, and read early themselves. Reading with kids who already know how to read helps them feel close to caretakers, understand the world around them and be empathetic citizens of the world.

- Music

  Science has shown that when children learn to play music, their brains begin to hear, and process sounds that they could not otherwise hear. This helps them develop 'neurophysiological distinction' between certain sounds that can aid in literacy, which can translate into improved academic results for kids, teens, and adults. Music is extremely important in our lives and it is also a great factor to happiness.

~" To be in the memory of your children tomorrow; you must be present in their lives today. "

Fight for your life

There is a fight right around the corner just waiting for you, so you better learn how to fight. You must get up every morning and fight! Clawing and scratching! You must beat depression. You must beat anxiety. And you have to beat that little voice in your head that is telling you that you are not good enough. When I talk about fighting, I am not talking about people. I am talking about situations. I am talking about circumstances. I am talking about opportunities that sometimes you must fight for. Come on life let's fight! Come on job let's go! Come on career let us go! I am going to war!!!

That dream is not going to just sit there and wait for you to come get it. You must chase it. Like a woman possessed. You have to go get it. But to win fights you must have stamina. You must be ready to fight and bounce back. Punch and counter punch. Jab and jab back. Life is a series of fights. The worst thing you can do is run away from your fights. Life is a series of fights and if you ran away, you just ran away from your life. We must fight. We cannot lay down! When you lay down, you get run over.

When you are about to fight or you know a fight is coming, your adrenaline begins to pump. Your heart begins to raise. Your mind gets right and says I am going to win this battle sucker, you are going down! Some of you guys out there are fighting for your life, why? Because the doctor told you, you don't have a chance? You better not feel sorry for yourself. You better not lay down and quit. You better get up and fight. Because a happy spirit does a body like a good medicine
.
Fighting for the future, fighting for your dreams, fighting for success. When you come home raise your arms like a

champ. Sometimes in life you get caught with a good one. You did not see divorce coming. You did not see cheating coming. You did not see being fired coming. You have been sucker punched.

I have been there myself. I have been sucker punched before. I get seizures, I have had three strokes. I had to learn to walk again and I still have a left side deficit. I have had cancer. I live with a heart monitor because my heart has issues. But that does not mean I can stop fighting. You must get up baby! When you get sucker punched get up. If you get hit in the gut, get up. You must learn how to fight one battle at a time because you might not win the fight, but you must win the war. You must have the right attitude, the right mindset, the right mentality, because there's going to be a war and you can't quit, until you win!

~"When you think about your life, remember this: No amount of guilt can change the past, and no amount of anxiety can change the future!"
#Relax

The law of attraction

What do you want to do in life? Do you ask the universe for it?

So many of us choose our paths out of fear because what we really want seems possibly out of reach and ridiculous to expect so we never dare to ask the universe for it. Jim Carey once said; "remember that life doesn't happen to you, it happens for you". And how does he know? Well, his response was he did not know, but he was just making sound and that's the important thing. Hahaha... Well, just like Jim I am also making a sound. The sounds of the words that say you cannot give up on your dreams.

I believe that is what is important really. Letting each other know we are here for one another. Reminding each other that we are part of a larger self and asking the universe for what you might think is impossible.

Let us do an exercise.

TALENT.

On the count of three go ahead and say the word Talent. Say the word talent to yourself without opening your mouth. Without saying anything to the outside.

Ready? 1... 2... 3... TALENT

If you said it in your head correctly, without saying the word out loud the question to ask is: what voice was that? What voice just spoke? You just said the word talent without moving your mouth at all. And on top of saying talent, you heard yourself say talent. How can you hear yourself say talent and no single vibration of sound has happened? This puts a different perspective on what sound is and what memory is.

Memory is not in the brain. It is in the soul. The only thing you take after this life is your memories, or your knowledge, your experiences. That is the only thing you take. But if you said talent in your mind what voice spoke? That you heard but not with your ears because your mouth did not move. The ears did not hear it, the mouth did not move, but you spoke. And you heard yourself speaking?
If you close your eyes you can see this even better. What is the sight that can see your future? These two eyes do not see the future, these two eyes do not see the past and yeah you can see your past and you can see your future. You can see your past but what is the sight that can see beyond time? Hmmm...

This is an ancient meditation. In fact, I am not the flesh, I am the energy in the flesh, and this is proven, this is not fake, it is not religion. It is a fact that you can speak without moving your mouth. You can hear without ears. You can see without eyes. What happens when these eyes, this mouth, and these ears drop into the grave? These other senses are all you are left with. Death is an illusion, once you realize this you live your life more courageously.

No one wants to die before their time, so we try to protect ourselves. But know that this body is the limitation of you. This body is not your ultimate. The ultimate is that voice that just said talent. That voice that just said talent without nothing physically moving. That person is immortal. That person is not here with you.

Let us go deeper. The body is in three dimensions; Front and back, left and right, up and down. Oh, and time. That is a physical reality. So, what happens to in and out? What is in and out? Talent! Talent says... I exist without the body! So where is this other existence? Where is it? It is not here. This voice is in a completely different dimension. Just switch a little, talk to yourself more, affirm to yourself more, don't go saying I can't do this I can't do that. Go within saying IM THE GREATEST EVER! I have all my needs coming with speed.

I am a being of love, light, and knowledge. No weapon formed against me will prosper. Whatever it is you have to say, say it! This is how the Gods created this whole reality. Talent! Before there was a body there was this voice traveling in this voices dimension. To get here to the earth, the inner voice created this outer extension of itself to be in this dimension. Once you realize that you are not just in this dimension but also in another dimension, you now are free because whatever happens to you in this dimension is not your only reality.

See this is how Jesus was able to get beaten and brutalized and hung on the cross. He was not here! He was the talent. Inside he went to the inner man. Do what you want with the body, I am not here! Once you realize that level of consciousness where you identify yourself as the spirit and not as the flesh, you are the inner voice not the outer voice. Once you become your inner voice, now your outer voice has power. When you speak, it is not just a shell speaking, there is a being speaking through the shell and this is where you heal all sickness in your body.

This is where you command reality to work with you and it works according to your consciousness. Why? Because it is not the shell that is speaking, there is a real being in the shell that is speaking. And when a real being speaks, all nature and the universe respond. As I always say, it all starts with you.

~" There is no such thing as a hopeless situation. Every circumstance in your life can change."

Be strong, it may be stormy now, but it never rains forever

Have you ever felt like you are falling apart? Like time is just passing by and you are stuck in the same place? Well, I understand what you are going through. I have been there. Sometimes it takes some things falling apart for better things to fall into place. Sometimes it takes losing what you are settling for to remind you of what you truly deserve. It takes the most uncomfortable paths to lead your life to the most beautiful place. Believe me, I know it is hard, but you will never see the purpose of the storm until you see the growth it produces.

You will never see the purpose of someone leaving your life until you see it was the best for your life. You will never understand why you are going through what you are going through until you see the strength, the power, and the growth that it built inside of you. I need you to hear me, believe, and understand me. Yes YOU! Your current situation is not your final destination. This storm will eventually run out of rain. This struggle that seems to be lasting forever will eventually run out of pain. This hurt you, will turn you into the greatest you. This broken you, will turn you into the best you. Please let the hardest time of your life turn into your best life. Let these bad days create your best days
.

I need you to understand that just because something is over doesn't mean your life is over. Life is like a book, but this chapter is not your story and this moment is not your identity. This pain that you feel is not your life. This pain that you feel will become power. This weakness will become strength. Your confusion will become peace. Better things are coming for your life. Those tears will dry, your heart will heal, your mind will calm, and the storm will end. It will take time, but I promise you things will get better and everything you are going through will eventually turn to everything you made it through. Do not forget that every single day is a new beginning. Make today yours. It all starts with you.

~ *"The fun thing about life is, once you start taking note of the things that you are grateful for, you start to lose sight of the things that you lack. We are all affected by our past, but it is in our power not to let what we have done dictate what we will do".*

You must be hungry to succeed

I have always wanted to be in the medical field, so I took a course. I became a medical assistant, and of course now I want to work. I went on a job hunt, and along the way I turn a bit picky and decided I wanted to work for a specific hospital. So, I go to the hospital of my liking. When I am there, I bump into this man in the hallway that looks at me and says, "may I help you?" I say, "yes of course, I am looking for employment". He tells me, "well I can tell you this, they're not hiring here. But, if you're hungry enough anything can happen." I looked at him weirdly after his comment and said thank you. I went into the human resources department looking perfect for the job in the hospital I wanted to work for. But to my not so surprise, the supervisor tells me, "I'm sorry but we are not hiring at the moment."

I left and I came back the next day and I speak to the same supervisor and say, "Hi, how are you? Are you hiring?" She looks at me with a weird face and tells me, "didn't you come yesterday?" And I said, "Yes, I did." Then she looks at me with a weird face but tells me, "I apologize we are not hiring at the moment". I told her "OK! Thank you, I only came because I thought maybe someone could've been let go, or maybe someone was a temporary or maybe someone just didn't show up and quit." Again, she looks at me with a weird face, but I quickly turned around and I leave.

The next day came along and what did I do? I went to go get a job at the hospital that I wanted to work for. I speak to the same supervisor. She looks at me and says, "Ma'am I told you we are not hiring." I looked at her and said, "Well I was thinking maybe someone could've gotten fired." She said, "no one has been let go." Again, I said "OK! Thank you and sorry for any inconvenience."

We are on day number four. I go back to the hospital, and I go back to speak to the same supervisor again. Right then and there she looks at me and says, "Do me a favor, can you go grab me some coffee?" And I said, "Yes ma'am!" I went down and got her coffee and toast. I came back up, when I came up not only did, I get her the coffee and toast, I also got myself a job. I did not get the medical assistant position that I wanted but I was definitely working in the hospital of my choice. Now I am a step closer.

They place me in the Human Resources department giving me a floater position doing things that were not quite to my liking. I do not want to be closed in an office being someone's assistant. But it was ok, it gave me an opportunity and I stuck by it. The supervisor in the department I was in sends me to cover at another department in the hospital. When I arrive at the office they asked, "what did you study again?" I say, "I'm a medical assistant." They reply, "can you do me a favor, can you just cover the front desk while our rep arrives?" And I say, "not a problem." I sit at the front desk and start answering the phone.

I start taking care of business without training, without anything. They are bearing with me because I am only covering for someone else. The person in charge of the front desk returns and says, "thank you for covering." I respond, "you're very welcome, it was a pleasure." I get ready to go, and as I am leaving a doctor walks in needing assistance. He asks me if I worked there. If I was new. I tell him yes. He says, "great, come and assist me." Mind you I am fresh out of school so whatever he was asking me to do I knew. I knew what I was doing. I was hungry. After successfully assisting the doctor I turn to him and say, "Doctor I would like to properly introduce myself. My name is Joanne, and I am not an employee here. I was temporarily assisting at the front desk." And he responds, well "you are now". I was hungry.

I was so hungry that they fed me. I ate because it is what I wanted. This is the reason I am telling you; you must be hungry. If you are hungry you will succeed. I can assure you that. You can never give up. When they tell you no, turn it into a yes. If you are hungry you need to feed yourself. If you don't eat, how do you survive? Without food, without water, without eating. It is not possible because you are human. Do not take no for an answer. If they are not hiring, well they are going to start hiring. If you really want it, the moment you walk in that door they are now hiring. If you want something in life you have to stay hungry enough to go after it and eat it. Once you have done so, there will be nothing else to say than, bon appetite!

" Accomplishment is the greatest thing in life, and I disagree. The attempt to actually try to accomplish anything is actually what's great "

Moving On

There are times you feel that you cannot get over someone even if you wanted to. You will ask yourself, how is it that they are moving on and I am still stuck here? They are happy and I am still crying over them. How do I move on? Yes, it is hard. Yet simple.

First, you must really want to move on. It only depends on you. Then you must change their identity. Change their identity and I assure you that the identity that they have in your heart is pleasure. Understand that, that identity is something that just makes you feel good. But what happens when something makes you feel good? It becomes an addiction. It is like a drug and you have it around because it makes you feel comfortable. When something causes you pain you run from it right? That's why we do not stick our hands in the fire. Because it brings you pain, right?

That is when addiction happens. Even though it causes pain now, at the beginning you programed yourself to say this gives you pleasure. You say this makes me feel good. It relieves stress, and it makes me forget about my problems for the moment, so it is hard to break. And that is exactly what is going on in your life. You are addicted to this person. You are addicted to the feeling this person used to give you. You are addicted to the person that they used to be, that they no longer are.

You must break the cycle to break the habit. You are human, and because you are human, you are going to want to go back to that person. But when that happens, that is when you need to stop and realize that you are not going back to pleasure, but to pain. This person is pain, and that is when you must get in action and program yourself and say, I am not going back to pain! Do anything you have to do. Block them from everywhere. Change his name on your phone. Do whatever you have to do and repeat it to yourself.

Train yourself until their identity moves from pleasure to pain. When in your mind, your heart, your soul, everything you own sees him as pain, I promise you, that you will no longer want to walk towards his way. You will then have realized the difference in your life and what you had when that pain in disguise was around. Change their identity. This does not only go for relationships. You can apply this to anything you have ever become addicted to. Remember that it all starts with you.

~" Achievement is the greatest thing in life, and I don't agree. The attempt to try to achieve anything is the real achievement. "

It is not a figment of your imagination; some people just want to use you.

I have had many experiences with those who at times I have called a true friend. Some of us need to understand that some people do not come in your life to love you. They come into your life to use you. They do not come to bring to your life, they come to take from it. They do not see you as a person, they see you as an opportunity. I have been there. These are the types of people that do not love you for you. They love you for what they can take from you. They are not loyal to you. They are loyal to the benefit that comes with you. That is why they never show up no matter how many times you showed up for them. That is why they never offered help no matter how many times you offered to help them.

I believe its time you stop breaking your back for people that do not have yours. I have decided and I refuse to be used. Stop taking punches for people who will not take a punch for you. Stop keeping people in your boat that are not rowing with you. Stop being there for people who always disappear on you. I hate to say this but its simple facts. If they are not supporting, then they should not be important. Think about it. Just because someone is in your life, it does not mean they want the best for your life. Let me ask you this question. If your talent were not there, would they still be there?

If all you had to offer was friendship, would they still be around? I know you want their support; I get it. But understand that you do not need their support. I know it sucks when you find out that the ones you love the most will sometimes support you the least. I know it sucks to find out that the ones you did the most for will not even do the least for you. But do not let their lack of support create a lack of believe. Go out and get around those people that appreciate your talent, not just want to use you for it. Get around people who want to help you elevate your life, not just use you to elevate theirs.

I also get that you will look around and say, so then who is there to support me? There is a whole world out there waiting to support you. Do not let those that do not support you keep you from seeing that.

I am not going to sugar coat anything; I am going to be clear. When you finally remove these people from your life, because you will, they are going to try to paint a picture for the world that you are wrong when they were the ones that did you wrong. You need to understand this and please never forget it. Never feel guilty. Never feel guilty for cutting someone off when they handed you the scissors. Do not forget, if you want to make it happen, it all starts with you.

~*"If your actions do not prove the truth of your words, then your words are nothing more than lies. If they love you like they say, then they wouldn't treat you like they do. If words don't add up, it's usually because truth wasn't included in the equation. Actions always prove why words mean nothing. Words lie but actions don't."*

The only thing you should quit in Life

Life is not about perfection, is about progression. Just because you make a mistake it does not mean you are a mistake. Those people that judge us have imperfections too. They just hide theirs well. Stop allowing social media to make you hide who you truly are because you are trying to be something that you are not. Only to please people that can care less about you anyway. Take it from me, I am the perfect example of a walking mistake.

Quit accepting less. Life is too short to settle. Life is too short to just accept whatever. Do not lower your standards to reach someone at their level. If someone wants to truly be in your life, they will raise their standards to reach you in yours. Stop lessening yourself to make people feel comfortable. There is nothing wrong with knowing your worth or protecting your life. There is nothing wrong with guarding your heart. Only people that want to use you will make you think any different.

Stop measuring your life. Stop thinking you are not enough because your life does not add up to what the world wants you to be. Quit comparing your life. This is your life! Stop comparing your journey with someone else's journey. Do not allow society to put these labels on you. Stop thinking that you must look a certain way to be beautiful. Realistically, you are beautiful because of who you are. Stop thinking that you must have these certain number of followers or these certain amount of dollar bills in your bank account to be successful. Realistically, you are successful if you want to be. You are great because of who you are. When you do this, I can assure you that you are going to appreciate who you are.

✓ *Let's do the following.*
I learned this from someone that motivates me a lot as well and I would like to pay it forward. Grab a ruler or measuring tape. The point is to grab an object that measures. This will represent society. Now, cut it. Or break it with your hands. I want you to stop measuring your life and start appreciating it! You are going to keep this measuring tape where you can see it every day to let it remind you that you are more than enough.

What you need to reach success

Success...

I will start by telling you that I get seizures. I cannot drive. I had cervical cancer. I also have something called atrial flutter which is an abnormal heart rhythm caused by cardiac arrhythmia which can lead your heart to beat in an irregular pattern. Yes, it affects your heart. I have a loop recorder inserted near my heart that always gives the hospital access to monitor my heart. I randomly pass out. I have had three strokes and actively still have a left side deficit, although I control it well. I was placed in a rehab center where I received therapy. I was only able to stay the time that my insurance covered. When the insurance could no longer cover the inpatient therapy, they suggested I go to outpatient therapy. Guess what? The doctors could not find an outpatient center that would be covered by my insurance. I waited and waited. Time passed; I was running out of luck. No centers that took my insurance were found.

While going through this minor obstacle, I always kept a smile on my face. None of these things faced me. You know why? I had a goal. If you do not have a vision of where you are going. If you do not have a goal where to go, you drift around and never end up anywhere. Seventy four percent of the people in America hate their job. Most people do not like what they are doing. They are not doing it because they had a goal and followed the goal. They just aimlessly drift around and look for job openings, so they get the job just because they need to work. Only a quarter of people really enjoy what they are doing in life. I have had doctors ask me, "How is it that after all you have been through and currently still going through, you always have a smile on your face? There are others out there with your same condition yet look so sour in the face. Why is that?" My answer is simple, "I'm shooting for a goal." Every therapy I take gets me closer to accomplishing that goal. I am going to take this goal, this vision, and turn it to a reality.

I currently go to the gym daily and continue to give myself therapy. Every single set that I do, every repetition of weight that I lift, will get me a step closer to turning this goal into a reality. I could not wait on the insurance to call me. I could not wait on the doctors to find something for me. I remembered what I had to do. I remembered everything I learned at the rehab center and put it to work. My insurance was not going to stop me. I decided that I was going to be my own new rehab center. Visualizing your goal and going after it makes it fun. You must have a purpose no matter what you do in life. I worked my ass off. I never stopped and I have not stopped. There is no magic pill. There is no magic out there. You cannot get around it, you cannot buy it at the store. You must work and work hard. Yes, it is hard, but you must work.

It drives me crazy when people say they don't have enough time. They don't have enough time to improve their life. Either if it is physically improved or mentally improved. Imagine you reading one hour a day about history. How much would you learn after three hundred and sixty-five hours in one year? Imagine studying the history of musicians or composers. How much would you know? Imagine if you worked on a business that you wanted to develop every day for one hour. Imagine how further along you would go.

There are twenty-four hours in one day. We sleep about six hours a day, so we still have eighteen hours. Oh, if anyone out there is thinking "well, I sleep eight hours or more" … Well, sleep faster! With eighteen hours a day the average person works from eight to ten hours. Let us assume it is ten hours. We have eight hours left. If you are busy traveling around for an hour a day or maybe two hours a day, you still have six hours left. What do you do with the six hours? Maybe eat a little bit. Talk a bit to people etc. Or even maybe smooch for a little bit. You can see how much time you have available if you organize your day. You have got to work hard.

I don't like plan B. We have so many doubters. Which those are the no sayers to me! If so many of those people did not say "no, you can't do it", it is impossible! I mean, it's ok because we are humans and we just turn off. You must remember to turn your No into a Yes. You can't do it means you can do it. Yes, it is possible to do that amongst all the negative people around you. When you start doubting yourself its dangerous. What you are basically saying is if my plan does not work, I have a fallback plan. I have plan B. Now you start thinking about plan B. Which means that every thought that you put into plan B is withdrawing from those thoughts and energy you put into plan A. It is important that you understand that we function better if there is no safety net. Plan B becomes a safety net and says that if I fail, then I fall and get picked back up because I have something else there and it will protect me. That is not good. People perform better when there is no safety net. Even in sports, people perform better and everything else when there is no plan B.

I have never really had a plan B. I simply make a full commitment to myself to reach that goal. I am going to be a leading woman no matter what it takes. I will do the work. I started my healing process, got to work, and started training myself over and over until I got it. For me, it is extremely dangerous to have a plan B because you are cutting yourself off from the chance of really succeeding. Another reason people like having a plan B is because they are worried about failing. What if I fail? Then I won't have anything else. Well, let me tell you something, do not be afraid of failing because there is nothing wrong with failing. You must fail in order to climb the ladder. There is no one that does not fail. That is not possible. It is ok to fail. What is not ok is to fall and stay down. Whoever stays down is a loser. Winners will fail and get up. Fail and get up, and then fail again and get up again. Just always get up. That is a winner.

We all lose. We all have lost, and this is ok. Do not worry about losing because when you are afraid of losing you stay frozen. You get stiff. You are not relaxed. To perform well in anything, weather if it is at your job or even just your thinking, it would only happen when you are relaxed. So please, RELAX. Go all out and give it everything you have got. That is what it is all about. Do not be afraid to fail.

~ Failure is simply an opportunity to begin again, this time more intelligently. Don't be afraid to fail because only through failure do you learn to succeed. Take chances and make mistakes. That is how you grow. Pain nourishes your courage. You must fail in order to practice being brave. Keep trying. Keep fighting. Believe in yourself!

Those people don't care about you

I have a question for you. Why do we care so much about the people that do not care about us?

Why do we care so much about people that do not even know us?
These people that will not be there in the hard times. These people that will not be there in our struggles.

Why do we care about these people that will not even call you or ask you how you doing?

Why do we care about what they think?

Why do we live our life to be validated so much by strangers?

Why do we let people or even social media dictate how we feel about ourselves?

Our self-esteem or worth depends on if they like it or not. What they comment about. What they say. Who cares?! Those people are not going to be there when times get hard. Those people do not even like you. Half of them don't! Those people do not care about you so why are you placing value on what they think? Why are you living a life to impress them? Painting the perfect picture or finding the perfect filter. Doing obvious things to impress them.

Why???

You need to place value on the people that have loved you on your worst. Those are the people that deserve to be there when you are at your best. Not people that just love the fake you. That just love the perfect you. These people that are just waiting for you to mess up so that they can pick you apart. So that they can expose all your flaws yet, we live for these people.

Why?

Maybe it is time to log off on finding validation through social media and log on to focusing on the people that truly value who you are. I have tons of supporters and I guarantee you that there are very few that actually care about me. It is rare for me to get a call from someone just to know how I am doing or if I am ok. It is rare for me to get a call from someone saying, is there anything that I can do for you?

I get it. It is the life that I live, so I get it. But I understand where my focus and support truly is. I do not share everything about my life to them. It is my personal life. I do not have to share every thought. I do not have to share every problem. I do not have to share every situation. I do not have to let anybody into my life except the people who deserve to be there.

You protect your home. You do not let just anyone come into your home if you do not know them. You do not let them mess it up because you know they do not care about it. What is the difference with your life? Stop letting people in on everything that you are doing. You do not have to share every single thing you do in your life with anyone. Keep some things for you. You do not have to share that you are having relationship problems to the world. Work on it instead of sharing it. Update your problems to God and not to people.

Finding validation in them? In people that do not care. Why? You have already been validated. What they say, what they like, or what they comment are the things that make you feel special. Those are not the things that are special about yourself. You already know who you are. Stop letting people make you feel different.

~"Ignoring the red flags because you want to see the good in people will cost you later!"

Get ready to take action

Don't wait to be ready. Jump on it and take action. Do not ever hold yourself back by planning every detail. Start by taking action since you like to plan every little detail of what you are doing. Once you take action then plan the rest. Allow yourself to take imperfect actions. I am challenging you to create a timeline and see what happens. It is simple. Think less and act faster.

Have you been waiting for the perfect moment to get started on something? I know you have that grand idea or project in the back of your mind that you have been putting off for the past few days, weeks, months, or maybe even years. I hate to break it to you, but there is no such thing as the perfect moment. So many of us wait around until the perfect moment to act. We hold ourselves back from taking action on the things we think about repeatedly.

The thing is, we are only wasting time if we are thinking about doing things instead of actually doing them. You only have so much time and energy to spare. I do not want you wasting it all on thinking instead of doing. As someone who loves to stay in my comfort zone, I get that it is ridiculously scary to take risks. But you deserve to do the things you want to do my friend.

Let's talk about taking action before you are ready. I am going to share how I took the leap into self-employment before I was ready, as well as how you can stop holding yourself back and take imperfect action. I hope these words will give you a kick in the butt to start what you have been putting off.

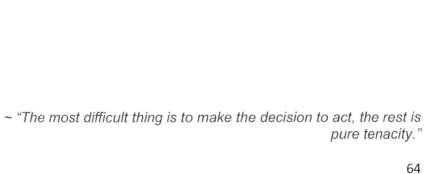

~ *"The most difficult thing is to make the decision to act, the rest is pure tenacity."*

Being ready is a myth

I know how easy it is to get caught up in your own thoughts instead of taking action on them. It is easy to replay the same thoughts about whether you should do something or not because you are unsure of how it is going to work out. With any of the major decisions I have made in my life, I have never really felt ready to do any of them. I mean, when do we ever feel fully ready to do anything? If you do feel ready, you probably waited too long to get started.

I think its bullshit to convince ourselves that we should feel ready before we do anything. This only holds us back from taking action. Instead, we need to be okay with the concept of taking imperfect action and figuring out the details afterward. I always hear "I don't feel ready for this race." Truth is, that no one is ever ready for a race. No one is really ever ready for anything in life even when we think we are. A new job, a new baby, a death, marriage, or losing our virginity - but we do them anyway - some with more enthusiasm than others.

The line of ready is like an asymptote that you will never really reach. As soon as you think you are close you will immediately think of some way you could get better. Or you realize how far you have come in your fitness, and that as of right now you can build on this and be even more ready for this same race next year. You can be slightly closer or further away from being more ready than another person. But you can also be less fit and get more ready in a shorter amount of time with wise training, nutrition, and rest. If we all reach the same point of readiness, close to the asymptote of actually being ready. What is it that separates the top finisher from the rest? That gap between ready and what we are, is all mental.

"From different desires, often the deadliest pain arises"

Taking imperfect actions

People always ask me how I knew I was ready to take my blog fulltime and become my own boss. The answer is that I wasn't. My original plan was to obtain seniority in my full-time job at the hospital I indeed loved to work at. But things did not exactly go as planned. I went into work on September 24th, 2017 and as I walked in, my boss calls me into the office and says, "We need to talk." My boss told me that she loved my work ethics but that as much as she did not want me to leave (she had no choice but to let me go); she stated "I was a great employee but that my health issues were interfering with my position".

I went into panic mode about what I was going to do. I did not feel ready to take that leap in the slightest. At that point, my options were to do self-employment or try to find another job. I did not want another 9-5 job. I came up with a new action plan: I would give myself three-month probation period to make self-employment work. I didn't know what I was going to do in those three months, but I decided this would be my trial period. Over those three months, I started offering life coaching services. I did not feel ready to do that either because I was still in the midst of my graduate school program for coaching.

Regardless, I shared with the world that I would be coaching soon. Somehow the stars aligned, and I booked my first client in New York City. Not only did I book my first client, but I got the opportunity to expand my horizons by traveling. Ever since, I have been figuring out the details along the way. I have had my ups and downs, but I am still making it work. If I had not had that push to take action when I was not ready, I would not be where I am right now. The truth is that things often fall into place if you give them the chance.

"Tragedy is a tool for the living to acquire wisdom, not a guide to live."

Seize the opportunity

Take advantage of the opportunity when it is offered. Great opportunities don't come every day. Take the chance, remember that it is not who you are that holds you back. It is who you think you are not. Open your eyes! Be alert! All you must do is learn to recognize them. A lot of the opportunities given to you in life are obvious. But many others are hidden. Your success does not depend on your abilities, it depends on your determination to grasp the opportunity that is presented to you so, what are you waiting for?

You have not because you ask not. Stop limiting what you asked God for because you are basing it on your current situation. Do not restrict your blessings from God just because you do not know how to ask. Many of you are willing to stay with someone that betrayed your trust. I was so terrified that I was willing to accept being treated less than I am. I know I am not alone in this because we have convinced ourselves that being disrespected is better than being alone. But you have the power. There is power in rediscovering your own voice.

Have you ever found out about an amazing opportunity (like a chance to be the head of your department), only to realize that you are terrified to try? I have been in all these risky scenarios, so I know how intimidating they can be. Risk-taking doesn't guarantee that you will attain your desired result. However, there are a few things you can do to optimize your chances of succeeding when an opportunity comes your way.

It takes time to achieve expertise. To be precise, it takes about ten thousand hours of practice to become a true proficient. This is no small investment of your life energy. As such, it pays to spend time thinking about the kind of opportunities you want to prepare yourself for.

If you are an advocate, what do you want to say to those senators? Start saying it now, even if you are speaking to an empty room at first. If you are a figure skater, what elements do you want in your Olympic program? Start practicing those elements every day.

Once you have seriously invested yourself and have discerned what kind of opportunity you are looking for, keep your eyes open, because opportunity has a strange way of showing up once you have prepared. Said opportunity may be unexpected (the best ones are), but if you have put in the time beforehand, you can seize the opportunity when it arises. Nevertheless, it is also essential. You can choose to a see a screw-up as a reason to hope, an opportunity to grow. The best skaters take a fall and keep going with a smile. They have the ability to consider the audience perspective.

It is tough to smile right after you have made a mistake, but think of it this way: Is there anything an audience loves better than a good comeback? "Our best days often start out as our worst days. And our greatest opportunity is often disguised as our biggest problems." So, do you dare? I am all in. Who's with me? Let us SEIZE THE OPPORTUNITY.

~"When you don't understand what's going on in your life, all you have to do is close your eyes, take a deep breath and say, God, I know this is part of your plan, just help me get through it. God will then give you wings and not because you have passed, but for you to use them and prove that you are alive! It only takes one day at a time and do not forget that after all, it is tomorrow that worries about yesterday. Do not pray for a lighter burden, instead pray for a stronger back. God has a reason to allow everything that happens to you. We may never understand his wisdom, but we simply must trust his will! Believe." Have faith!

Be by yourself

Spending some time alone means being able to know yourself a little more. Give yourself some time. Do not ignore yourself so you stop settling for less. Remember you are going to make mistakes. Your life is not perfect, and it never will be. Continue to give your all anyway. Never let anything stand in your way of you achieving your goals and real happiness.

Most adults have spent a non-trivial amount of time being untethered to other people. Almost everyone has spent at least a few years being single or otherwise socially "alone" often due to relocating or starting over in a new place.

While some people get a lot of enjoyment out of these more independent years, for others, the absence of a stable social environment is an emotional struggle. If you are having a hard time feeling happy on your own, try the strategies listed below. They all have cognitive benefits, and none of them include dating.

1. Get emotionally on board with your aloneness.

   Alone-ness, in and of itself, is a neutral experience. It can be made a positive experience ("solitude" or "privacy") if you have embraced it and feel in control of it. It can be a negative experience ("loneliness" or "isolation") if you believe it means there's something wrong with you.

   The first step to being happy alone is to accept and embrace the fact that you are alone. It doesn't mean there is anything wrong with you. It doesn't mean you are unlikeable or unlovable. It simply means that, for now, relationships will not be the center of your world. And that is fine.

2. Develop a relationship with yourself.

   It is a mistake to think that you can only have a meaningful relationship with another person. The adage that "the most important relationship you'll ever have is with yourself" will never ring truer than when you are at a point of alone-ness.
   To strengthen your relationship with yourself, make an effort to get to know yourself better. Ask yourself: What do I really value in life? What do I need more of? What do I need to be done with? What is next for me?

   Once you know the answers to these questions, you can start providing yourself with the emotional support and encouragement needed to pursue your newly identified goals.

3. Let your passions run free.

   When you are in a committed relationship or constantly around a lot of people, you may notice that your list of "passions" starts to conform to what those around you enjoy. For example, if your boyfriend loves wine, you may find yourself suddenly more passionate about wine than you otherwise would be.

   While this is not at all a bad thing, time to yourself creates an opportunity to explore some of your less mainstream (or less "impressive") passions. Want to binge on all the Harry Potter books? Do it! Want to try out every sushi place in the state? Why not? This is the time to do it! You are alive.

4. Make plans with yourself.

   One of the more difficult things about being alone is the absence of regular events to look forward to. When you are in a relationship, it's easy to plan a regular date night. When you have a strong circle of friends, it's easy to arrange recurring Saturday or Sunday brunch. When you are alone, it is harder to establish these types of routines.

   To counteract the "no plans" blues, pick out some things you like to do and then build them into your day in a predictable way. For example, walk to your favorite coffee shop every morning and take a steaming hot bath every night. By creating your own routines, you will introduce that "I'm looking forward to that" feeling back into your life.

5. Get physical affection where you can.

   Neuroscience has shown that physical touch is extremely important for happiness and well-being. For obvious reasons, this area of life can become sorely lacking when you are alone.

   To avoid the negative effects of physical alone-ness, give special attention to building physical affection into your life wherever you can. One way to do this is through hugs. If you meet up with even a casual acquaintance, be sure to end the encounter with a nice long hug. You will instantly get a rush of happy chemicals in the brain.

6. Make yourself proud.

One of the beauties of being alone is that you can live by your own standards. When you are not beholden to other people, it is easier to stop living by other people's expectations of what you should be doing. This creates an opportunity to get clear on what you really in your heart expect from yourself.

Knowing what you expect from yourself allows you to start putting these expectations into action. With some effort, you can meet your own expectations and make yourself proud.

If and when you find yourself socially alone, use these strategies to start seeing your situation as an opportunity. It is time to grow and become the person you really want to be. The truth is you will not be alone forever. And when you start re-connecting with people, you will cherish the memories of your time alone.

~"Do what you think is right for you, steal a kiss, laugh, cry, seek company, or be alone or I don't know, but do it and you'll see how the world fits perfectly for you."

The World as an Introvert

It seems today at least in the U.S. there must be something wrong with you if you are alone. We praise the extroverts. Those who know how to handle themselves in a crowd, the ones with vast network of friends. We think working in groups and on teams is the only way to find the answer to a problem. That two heads are better than one. That collaboration is the only way of the future. But the truth is almost half of the world does not agree. I do not feel that way. Sometimes, the rhetoric gets so loud I wonder what is wrong with me when I don't feel like going to parties, or working on big teams, or being the center of attention.

You see your friends going out and wonder what is wrong with you when you want to stay in. You see them collaborating on planning trips together and wonder if there is something wrong with you because you prefer to stay alone. But there is nothing wrong with you. You are an introvert. And, according to some statistics, there is about a 50% chance that we are all too. If you are an introvert, welcome to the club. There are not any meetings because you prefer to work alone, but you can at least take some solace in knowing you are not the only one who feels the way you do.

Being an introvert does not mean you do not enjoy going out or having friends or being the center of attention occasionally. It only means that it is not where you get the most value from your life. Being "turned on" and in social mode is fun for me, but others can only take in limited quantities. There are people that work in a team, but you cannot ask them to brainstorm because they will not come up with anything useful. However, if you leave them alone to think awhile, you might be surprised at what they accomplish. If you want your introvert friend to go out with you and your friends, invite them somewhere quiet where you all can talk. Not everyone is the same and we all get to accept that.

If you are an extrovert like me, do not assume there is no value in this for you. The same way I can enjoy myself in a big group, you may find you can also enjoy yourself… all by yourself. There is great value in being alone. And handling it well is a beautiful thing. At the very least, it is a useful life skill. You cannot always control when there will be someone there for you. So being able to happily conduct yourself alone is an important part of being alive.

"Everything that irritates us from others leads us to an understanding of ourselves."

"Pain is inevitable, but suffering is optional"

"Pain is inevitable, but suffering is optional". These words were said by Buddha after years of learning and meditation. He was wondering if suffering is really something we can choose. The word suffer comes from the verb "suferre." Ferré means carry or bear. Both suffering and pain are part of life. Although sometimes we suffer needlessly, we suffer because of our imagination and fear. We imagine things that do not happen.

The origin of emotional pain consists of four things:

- Unexpected change
- Fear
- Disappointment
- Accepting reality

I will provide you with the following tips, so you leave suffering aside.

1. Learn to manage pain as it allows us to grow.
2. Accept that the only constant thing in life is change.
3. Get ready for a huge change during your life.
4. Do not confuse the possible with the probable. Thanks to pain we can foresee and avoid future complications.
5. Do not anticipate what has not happened yet.

"Pain is inevitable, but suffering is optional."

~" The only antidote to mental suffering is physical pain."

Invest in yourself

Before you invest in a business and want to develop a project remember the following sentence by Tom Schreiter- "Invest first in yourself, unless you're a bad investment". By investing in yourself, it will be the best business you will ever do in your life.

To develop your business, you first need to develop your skills. The safest way to achieve a better quality of life is by being more productive and developing your goals. Achieving your goals is to set aside a part of your income for personal and professional development. This will give you the following benefits:

- Increase confidence and self-esteem so that you have a better quality of life.

- Investing in yourself does not have any risks. I can tell you that you have nothing to lose. Everything you learn, everything you do wrong, and everything that happens to you is profit, so it is the only investment that has no risks. I assure the bank cannot give you a better deal.

- Everything you learn is in you, and you can use it at any time. You will have greater economic benefits. According to Benjamin Franklin if you empty your pocket in your mind, your mind will fill your pocket.

What are you waiting for? You got nothing to lose. You got this!

~" The best investment you can make is in yourself. The more you learn, the more you are going to win"

Don't be a fool

People need to understand, you cannot compete where you do not compare. You cannot make a person who does not give a shit jealous. You cannot speak about anyone when you do not have your things together. You only make yourself look dumb when you try to make someone else look stupid. You know you are desperate when you try to give life to a dead situation. If you expect the world to be fair with you because you are fair, you are honestly fooling yourself. That is like expecting the lion not to eat you because you did not eat him.

Suddenly, they stopped talking to you. So be it, don't trip. God will sometimes cut an infection to keep it from spreading. The only people you owe your loyalty to are those who never made you question theirs. Maybe you believe you are a nobody at this moment, but well, get up and conquer your goals and I assure you; you will turn out to be like no other.

If the people who are trying to make this world worse are not taking the day off, how can I? Do not run away from your bullshit. Embrace it and become better. If you do not like where you are, move. You are not a tree.

Be thankful for all those negative people in your life, they will show you exactly who you do not want to be. Real friends talk shit to your face and say nice things behind your back.

Every time you date someone with an issue that you must work to ignore, you are settling. Never Settle. Never explain yourself to anyone. You do not need anyone's approval. Live your life and do what makes you happy. Sometimes what really defines someone is what they will not do. People with the worst past create the best future. Do not forget that you are human. It is ok to have a meltdown, just do not unpack and live there. Cry it out and then re-focus on where you are headed.

I tell you about my past, and it is never because I want you to feel sorry for me, but so you can understand why I am who I am. If they don't have the common decency to respect your time, effort or presence then let them get used to your absence. It is about that simple.

"Having a good heart attracts beggars, liars, users, takers and ungrateful people."
#BeCareful

Unconditional Love

Parents need to stop having certain expectations for their children and let them be who they are. Your son or daughter needs your unconditional love. Most people have lost sight of exactly what that means. It means that nothing a child does can make love stop. That is why it's unconditional.

As parents we must teach our children to grow up to be honest, responsible, intelligent, kind, respectful, humble, courteous, courageous, open-minded, independent, loving, and compassionate. These are the qualities that must matter. Not if your son prefers ballet over soccer or man over woman. Not if your daughter likes to wear baggy pants instead of miniskirts. Or if she is attracted to other women or a white or black man. We raise our children to be a certain way. The fact that they do not grow following all our ground rules does not mean you failed as a parent.

It simply means that it is your child's life, not yours. They come to this world to choose the things that they like and prefer. Stop turning your back on them or feel embarrassed because they do not follow your rules, or they are not what you want them to be. Stop treating them badly simply because they are not what you are. Teach them to be good people. That is what this world really needs. Teach them what really matters. Love your children unconditionally and support them.

I am me, my life is mine, and you are living yours. I do not criticize you even if you live full of defects. As a daughter the only thing that interests me is that my parents are happy at any cost. As a parent I am going to make a difference.

Give it... its unconditional love.

~" *Hate is for slackers, strong people love, and love a lot!*"

Your value

Observe and discover the value that you give yourself. This is not about math so do not be alarmed.

What is the value of this bill?

Correct, $20. If I fold this bill in half what is its value now? Half?

No, it is still $20. Right?

If I grab this bill and drown it in a glass of water and then punch it. What would be its value then? It is still the same, right?

How about if I pass it from hand to hand? If I start to speak badly to it, and start saying ugly things to it? For example, "you serve no purpose, you're so ugly and worthless." What is the value now?

It is still $20, right?

Last one. How about if I spit on it, what is its value now? The same?

You are telling me that this bill that we already punched, hit, drowned, and even spit on still has the same value now? Yes, it is still worth $20.

If you noticed, the value of the bill never changed no matter what we did to it. Even though we insulted it, spit at it, hit it, and even dunked it in water, its value never changed. I write about this because it is a lesson, we must all apply to our lives. We are like a bill. With a high value, and we cannot let a situation or circumstance define us and make us feel that we are worthless. Not a family member, not your boss at work, not anyone. Do not ever feel worthless. Even if anyone calls you dumb or says you are not smart enough. Nothing or no one can tell you that you are worthless or less than what you really are.

You are like this bill. Remember it. No matter what they do or say you will always have your value. You will go through situations that without a doubt will affect you, of course. And it is going to be hard to get out of your struggles. But know that that means that you are alive. You have life. Keep fighting for your dreams and goals in this life. We are not in this world just to survive.

It is amazing how people let other people decide what their value is. The next time you feel you are worthless remember this $20 bill. Remember that you, as this bill, already have your value assigned to you. Even though they tell you that you are worthless. That you are not ready. That you need more. That there is someone better than you or maybe you are too pretty or too ugly. You are still worth the same. Your situations and circumstances are not going to define you. You know what will define you? The attitude that you are going to take to grab the reins of your life and give a turn to that situation. I invite you to use this as inspiration for you to start creating a change every time you feel bad.

I am not going to lie; life hits you hard. I am not going to tell you that it is not going to hurt when they shout mean things to you. When they speak to you ugly, or when you are mistreated. I know it is going to hurt you and a lot. But guess what? When you get up, I am sure you are not going to make the same mistake twice. Not only that, but you will also keep preparing for what is to come. You are worth too much to let anyone define what your own value is. We come to this world to create incredible things.
As they say, sometimes money is just a means to help you live. Money does not buy happiness, but it is a hell of help. You are like this bill. I am not saying you are worth $20. The moral of this message is that you are worth gold.

~"Get strength, courage and confidence with every experience in which you really stop to look fear in your face. You have to do what you think you can't do."

Six psychological tricks to be attractive without being pretty

I am not going to talk about fashion. I am going to teach you why being attractive has nothing to do with having a pretty face or having the best body in the world. Of course, there are people who have both and do well in love. But I ask you a question, by any chance do you have a friend who is genuinely nice, very respectful, and somewhat attractive? That person that everyone wants to be with. They might not be the most pleasant person physically maybe, but that person has something that makes you love them. This type of person has personality, and they end up arousing the curiosity of wanting to know them. At the end of the day having a great personality speaks of having confidence in yourself. When you know who you are and what you want, you attract more people. Attraction is not physical, attraction is mental. Beware, there is no correct answer, we all like different things. Which is good because there is someone for everyone. I am going to give you six tricks to attract the person you like by being yourself.

1. You must be unique, create your own personality, be authentic, and empathize with the person that will make you feel good.

2. Mindset. Someone who is very insecure is automatically reflected in the way they treat other people. For example, when a person does not groom, does not brush their teeth well, or does not fix their hair says a lot about that person. It means that they do not have much self-esteem. It also means that they do not have a winning mentality. To have a winning mentality you need to have high self-esteem.

3. Listen to others. The most attractive thing in people is when you end up really listening to them. And no, I am not telling you that you have to listen to them, it is only when you really care genuinely that they will see the fact that you are truly worried about them. The next time someone has a conversation with you, instead of you just saying I understand you, form an opinion. Challenge them and that will speak much better of you.

4. Project confidence that can be reflected automatically if you are a person who is jealous and obsessive with your partner. A person who has confidence on themselves does not go around fighting with their partner over anything. He/she is a person who knows that they are worth enough to be respected so they expect the same change.

5. Be natural. At the end of the day you must be yourself. You cannot be projecting a person who does not exist. Why? Because eventually the person will get to know you and if what you say does not match with what you do, you will have a serious problem and at this point you will probably already be unattractive to the person you have conquered.

6. Physique. It is always important to maintain a physique which you identify and can be loyal to. I am not talking about what you see in the magazines of how it should be. I am referring to being you, that physique that defines who you are, how you are, and what you like.

There is this extremely attractive person. The attractive type society loves. But this person is very mean to their partner and family. He or she is also often rude which ends up being that although at first, they might be extremely attractive to the eye, he or she ends up being the worst person you could have met. You completely lose the attraction.

You can apply these tricks starting today and you will not only be more attractive, but you will also make a good impression. Remember that most of the time we judge people by the first thing we know about them. If we see one good impression, then we will probably stay with that judgment. But if it becomes bad that means you have been pretending, leading your partner to finding it harder to trust or fall in love again. If at any time you have feel that you have not been attractive enough for the person who has stolen your heart, it is important that you apply these tips and you will see a great change in your life.

~"If someone tells you you're not beautiful, turn around and walk away, so they can get a great view of the beautiful movement of your rear end."

Have you ever been a full day in silence?

You can hear yourself breathing...

Just a reminder in case your mind is playing tricks on you today, you matter. You are important. You are loved. Honestly, your presence on this earth makes a difference whether you see it or not. Never think that what you have to offer is insignificant. There will always be someone out there that needs what you have to give, just always know your worth.

When someone treats you like you are just one of many options, help them narrow their choice by removing yourself from the equation. Sometimes you must try not to care, no matter how much you do. You can mean almost nothing to someone who means so much to you. It is not pride. It is self-respect. Love yourself daily.

Do not give part-time people a full-time position in your life. Know your own value and what you have to offer. Never settle for anything less than what you truly deserve because I can clearly tell you that you are worth beyond a thousand reasons why. You cannot be perfect, but nobody is perfect. What I can tell you is that there is nobody in this world, like YOU!

~"Live as if you were going to die tomorrow, learn as if you were going to live forever."

It is you they don't click with

People fall in love. I assure you they know when they are hooked with a person they like. Just as they know what it is to love. They give flowers and gifts. They are also detailed and know how to show love. They also know the difference between having sex and making love.

What happens here is that the combination of the two of you does not add up. And that is what's killing you. They are not made of iron, they feel. The problem you are having is that they do not love you. What you have left to do is walk out with dignity because people with dignity do not kneel. You have not lost anything because the winner is not who leaves. But who leaves, forgets, and starts over. Continue going straight even if you stumble along the way because these are life experiences.

They do not love you and what? Nothing will happen. As I stated, they are not ironman, they feel. You are simply the one they do not click with. They are not your match. Let go.

~" Love might be blind... But you see how much their eyes brighten when they see you."

You are a badass

You are a badass, recognize it. If your ex after ten years still calls you, texts, or appears in places that you frequently go to, I can tell you that they have not surpassed you. If they are still following your every move, they have not surpassed you. If they still do not understand that you really do not want nothing with them, they have not surpassed you. And may not surpass you for a while. You must recognize at this point that you are a badass. You are loved massively, furiously, unconditionally.

The universe is totally freaking out about how awesome you are. It wants to give you everything you desire. It wants you to be happy. It wants you to see what it sees in you. Stop doubting your greatness

COMMANDMENT # 11
Don't put up with any cheating or lying human body just so your kids could live with a father/mother.

~" A disappointment is nothing more than a situation that helps you get out of the wrong place."

No competition

You can eat a lot of shit when you want to. Excuse my
French. Have you ever seen Diosa competing with
someone? Never right? I am going to help you get the devil
full of stupidity out of you.

Your man or girl left you. They left you for some ratchet ass
person that you know is useless. The first thing you must do
is thank God because he freed you from this person. They
are where they must be. Wallowing in the mud with the pig
they deserve in their life. You were too much for them
anyhow. Look at things from another point of view. You are a
gold mine that deserves to be flattered twenty-four seven.
He/She was not what you deserved. You are like a diamond
so shake it off. Feel good about yourself because you, like
me, have no competition. Pigs are dirty and full of mud and
you are not there, are you? Shall I say more?

No matter what world or industry you are in, it can be easy to
think of your environment as cut-throat or competitive.
Especially if the pressure to succeed is constant and
intense. Competing with and comparing yourself to others
can set you up for jealousy, stress, and exhaustion. Do not
waste your energy trying to change opinions. Do your thing,
and do not care if they like it. The ultimate victory in
competition is derived from the inner satisfaction of knowing
that you have done your best and that you have gotten the
most out of what you had to give. There is competition at
every phase of your life. The day we start thinking about it,
you lose your peace of mind. Which is why you should not
compete with anyone.

The biggest competition should always be yourself. Never
look to follow others or pull them down. Plan to test your own

boundaries. Success is a peace of mind which is a direct result of self-satisfaction in knowing you made the effort to become the best that you can become. Your life is your own unique journey. It is unlike a journey any other person, before you or after you, will ever take.

Do your work with your whole heart, and you will succeed. There is so little competition. To me, teamwork is the beauty of our sport, where you have five acting as one. You become selfless. Personality begins where comparison leaves off. Be unique. Be memorable. Be confident. Be proud. Always remember that the only person you should try to be better than is who you were yesterday.

~"Do your job with all your heart and you will succeed, there is very little competition."

Stop searching, and allow them to find you

Stop seeking. I am begging you to stop the search. I finally discovered how everything works and that is why I want to reveal the secret that nobody wants to share. I am going to give you some advice, grab something to write and take notes.

- Stay with whoever treats you well, even if sometimes you are a disaster.

- Stay with whoever looks for you and seeks to be part of your day to day.

- Stay with whoever listens to you and seeks to be part of your life.

- Stay with the one that makes you feel good about yourself.

- Stay with whoever rebuilds you and seeks to improve you.

People attractive to the eye are many. But who is attractive to the heart? That is unique, so choose well. I want to give you these tips because I would have loved for someone to have given them to me. Listen well because these words can also end up changing your life.

Stop looking, there is no answer. He does not talk to you because he does not care. He leaves your side because he is bored. He ignores you because there is someone else. Did you understand that? Should I continue?

Don't look for who don't look for you. Do not love who does not love you. Most of all, don't give everything for the one who does not give a penny for you. I have learned that there is no lack of time but there is lack of interest. Life is too short to run after someone who does not even walk for you. Why do you need to run behind them when they already know where you are? They have been inside your home and know all about your mysteries, yet they still don't look for you. Do not look and let them find you.

Do not look for something that they do not offer you. Don't ever beg. Love is not begged; gestures of love are given in a natural way. If he used to do things for you before and now, he doesn't, I feel bad telling you this but, it is over. Don't look and let the wind take away the unnecessary things in your life. Avoid all negative space from the positive in your life. I have learned the hard way. Stronger is not whom tolerates more but who is more capable of letting go.

If it doesn't bring joy to your life, let go!

If it doesn't brighten or build you, let go!

If it remains but does not grow, let go!

If he doesn't give recognition to your talents, let go!

If he doesn't caress you, let go!

If he doesn't boost your takeoff, let go!

If he says but doesn't act, let go!

If there's no place in his life for you, let go!

If he tries try to change you, let go!

If he starts imposing himself, let go!

If he simply doesn't add to your life, let go!

If when he's missing, you don't notice his absence, let go!

If everything is reduced to the physical, let go!

If he doesn't show what he says with facts, let go!

Do not look or go behind what they do not want to give you. Let go! I assure you that the fall will be much less painful than the pain of holding on to what could be, but it is not. Let it go. If he comes back, then you can ask yourself if it is probably for you or not. Stay open to the possibility that you may find those people who want to be part of your life in a healthy way.

Quit searching. I recommend that you allow them to find you. It is not about who is waiting for you, but who is looking for you. It is not about who likes you, it is about who stands by you. It is not about who loves you, it is about who shows you. Don't look for who does not look for you. Do not want the one who does not love you. Mainly, do not give everything for the one who does not give anything for you.

Tattoo these words to your mind and heart. You will never know if your partner is faithful. Matter fact, you will never know if he really loves you. Or know if he tells you the truth even while looking into your eyes. You just must trust, and if something goes wrong, your own destiny will show you that that person was not the right person for your life. Enjoy the moments that they can give you. At least you were happy, and you did not fail to commit. You will see how life will sort everything into place.

~"What belongs to you finds you."

Break up with anxiety

Anxiety...

Something that many people have a relationship with. Some know it and some don't. You have no love for anxiety, yet she seems to love you. Anxiety decides who you are or are not going to talk to. Anxiety is the reason they didn't talk to you. She is possessive. Anxiety doesn't like you talking to other people. She's irrational. Anxiety will make you take the long way home versus the shortcut to avoid people you've already seen twice because you don't know if it's ok to greet them for a third time. Due to anxiety you don't correct people that misunderstand you. You just go with it because being understood is what you wanted, but maybe ignoring the fact that they didn't understand you was what you needed. So, you say Thank you. Anxiety makes you play a roll, a roll that takes a toll and makes you believe that since your boyfriend or girlfriend left you no one else will ever want you. Then you constantly wonder, what happens to a black person when they feel important. Will I make it? Will I be able to fly high? Anxiety is constantly reminding you how easy you are to crush. When you think you are pushing against her will, that's when you think she will kill. You don't vote alone; you and she decide your next step in life.

But NO, STOP, FIGHT! You need to fight her to gain control of your home, your sanity, come on, you can do it, don't crack. Breathe...

If your relationships do not work, I am sure it is because the other person does not know they are signing up for a threesome. How do you expect for anyone to live with both of you if you can't control who's controlling you? You must breakup with anxiety before you get with him or her. I understand you don't handle separation well but she's not the only relationship you can count on. Letting go will feel like being stuck in a ring forced to fight but you must be determined to knock her out. You and anxiety have learned to live together, and I can understand that. It is possibly the longest relationship you have ever had but it won't be the only relationship you will ever have. It is time to let go. You have life, you are up, you are here, and the time is now. WAKE UP!

~" You are going to get out of this and any other situation because people like you shine even with a broken soul."

With a bad movement you lose the Queen

Chess is very educational. One of the most important lessons in chess is that with one bad movement you can lose the queen. Do not be afraid to lose what you have never had. The problem with you is that you want to value what you no longer have under your control.

You will worry tomorrow when they are no longer in your present or your future. By that time, you will already be part of the past. What do you think of that? The problem with you is that you cannot control what you did before and that has you boiling inside but you do not value what you have in your life either.

Take notice of everything that makes you happy. Take notice of how much you smile when you are around it. All the positive impacts it has on you. Open your eyes to everything you have. Do not wait any longer because tomorrow might be too late. Lastly, remember that you do not have to lose something to value it.

You have the power to see what is around you right now: value it and enjoy it because I am sorry to tell you that the people you love will go away one day. Your friends will not be your friends, your kids will start their lives, your job will end, and that is just the way it is.

Take the reins and make everything worth it. Make it so everything you have now stays in your memory forever. Do not wait until you lose it to realize how important and valuable it was. Either you are in or you are out.

Checkmate!

~*"Tears are perhaps the most selfless friends of our lives."*

Life on and be yourself (Don't change)

My father and I separated one day, he thought I was gay because I have a best friend that has stuck by me like glue till this day. She is my person, you know. I told my mother with a broken heart, feeling as if I was stuck in an empty space but, she thought the same way. Was I tripping? Yeah, but I guess she had a point at the end of the day.

My best friend is husky, and a little masculine looking. Now I have a bunch of stereotypes all in my head. If I were gay, I would think inspiration and music hate me. Have you read my YouTube comments lately? That is so gay gets dropped on the daily. We become so numb to what we are saying that it turns into a culture founded from oppression.

No, we do not have acceptance for them. Humans call each other fagots in ignorance that it is a word rooted in hate, yet our class still ignore it. The same hate that cause wars from religions, and gender to skin color. The same fight that lead people to walk-outs and sit-ins. Its human rights for everyone, there is no difference. Life on and be yourself. Did you read that correctly? LIFE ON AND BE YOURSELF!

My religion has taught me something else. If you preach hate while praying, those words are not blessed. The prayer you just put in has been poisoned. Majority of people are comfortable remaining voiceless rather than fighting for humans that have had their rights stolen. I might not be the like everyone else, but that is not important. I say, no freedom until we are equal.

Yes, I support it because our world is so hateful that some people would rather die than to be whom they are. It is a fact that no law is going to change us. WE have to change us!

Whatever God you believe in, we all come from the same one. If you strip away the fear, underneath it is all the same love.

~"Your character is like a tree and reputation as a shadow. Shadow is what we think of it, the tree is the real thing. You have to be real enough to be believable, but you don't necessarily have to be real enough to be real."

Don't get sick from a job

The most productive people in the world have more emotional intelligence than academic. This is serious and dangerous because what is affecting us the most in this society is emotional intelligence. We have people with a title, with a car, with a body but emotionally destroyed. If you do not have that you have nothing.

I recommend that you choose a career that brings you happiness through the connection with other human beings. Never neglect those who love you, no matter how much they pay you. No company will ever thank you for your family's destruction due to your excessive work in their company. Do not get sick from a job. You will always be substituted in a company. If you die now, the company will easily put another person in your place.

You must prioritize yourself to be able to produce money and somehow be a functional person. Always Do Your Best. Your best is going to change from moment to moment. It will be different when you are healthy as opposed to sick. Under any circumstance, simply do your best, and you will avoid self-judgment, self-abuse, and regret. There is one consolation in being sick, and that is the possibility that you may recover to a better state than you were ever in before. Often, our discomfort cannot be attributed to a specific source. It is simply a result of a career mismatch. Such was the case when I was working a grueling medical assistant position at the hospital. My left side deficit, aches, and tense muscles led me to book weekly therapy. (It was a very painful experience by the way.) It was not a person or project causing this. It was the job itself. But it took a process of elimination for me to realize that.

Set boundaries that serve you. I used to check my phone before my feet even hit the ground in the morning. If I had received a disparaging message, it set the tone for my whole day. I decided to make a rule for myself: No phone before breakfast. Take inventory of your own stress touch points and set boundaries that feel right to you. Try removing your phone from your bedroom entirely, which can take away the temptation to check in early or late and allows melatonin to work its magic. (The light emitted from your cell phone, often called "blue light" suppresses melatonin and stimulates your brain as if it were daytime.) The National Sleep Foundation recommends no screen time one hour before bed.

If stress at work is causing you real physical pain, and you feel strongly it will continue despite your best efforts, it might be time to go. Stop asking yourself (Is it time to leave?) you know the answer. I have watched many people seesaw when it comes time to make this decision, especially as it relates to walking away from a high-paying job. I often run them through this very simple pro/con exercise: Make a list of all of the things that work "gives" you; paycheck, benefits, status, but also headaches, stress, insomnia, strokes, panic attacks, etc. Then analyze to determine if the health costs outweigh the benefits.

If the answer is yes, walk away. If the answer is no, remind yourself that staying in a job is a choice. Despite its drawbacks there is power in that too. Do not wait to wake up paralyzed before reevaluating what your job is costing you. You are the architect of your career and your life. Own it. It all starts with you.

"If you feel like you lack the strength, change your lifestyle."

Six things you don't have to explain to anyone

Do not live giving so many explanations. Those who love you really do not need them. Here are six things that you do not have to explain to anyone.

1. If you need time alone, you don't have to ask for permission as long as they don't take it the wrong way.

2. You don't have to explain anything about the people around you, or the friends you have, the couple you chose, not even if you are single.

3. Your favorite things. What fills you is for you to enjoy personally.

4. Your career because it is your decision. Even if it is unconventional.

5. Your religious, Political, or spiritual beliefs. As long as you do not harm anyone you are free to believe in whatever you feel like believing in.

6. Your feelings. If you are not prepared to talk about something, nobody should force you.

Do not live giving explanations, we must be aware of what we do. There is no need to explain yourself to anyone. You have your own life, and it is only you who has the right to live it as you want. Just make sure that you have been true to yourself and you will not require explaining anything to others ever again. You do not take others approval to live your life. Isn't it? Remember that every person in this world will have different opinions about things, and thus, your outlook will vary from them immensely. Just make sure that you are happy for all that you do. Just make sure that you live your life in your own terms. Finally, your happiness is all that matters at the end of the day. You cannot make everyone happy all the time. It is more important to bother about your own happiness in the first place. You are what truly matters.

~" With you ALWAYS what with no one EVER"

Lift your self-esteem

You were born Queen/King. You were born to be great and shine more than the moon and sun put together. You must raise that self-esteem and learn to value yourself. You must get up from the ground and understand that if you do not love yourself nobody will do it for you. If your self-esteem is on the floor, you are subject to manipulation. You are a person that anyone can use and cheat at will.

You cannot let that happen because when you learn to love what you see in the mirror, there is not a soul that can destroy or hurt you. When it comes to your self-worth only one opinion truly matters - your own. Even that one should be carefully evaluated; we tend to be our own harshest critic. Everyone is good at something - from the job you do, to making others laugh - there is something you excel at. Many of us never take the time to acknowledge this fact to ourselves and tend to focus more on our weaknesses.

By providing positive reminders of our accomplishments and abilities, we can surprise ourselves with just how much we have achieved. It is a good idea to write down your achievements as they occur or as you remember them. Seeing them in black and white can provide an excellent reminder that we are far more capable and accomplished than we'd at first imagine.

Surround yourself with positivity. Ironically, one of the most effective ways of gaining self-confidence in yourself is to be surrounded with overwhelmingly positive people. Once you start doing this, you will find that their enthusiasm is catching, which can spark all kinds of ideas and plans in you too.

If you have a passion or interest, look for others who share it – even if it's to become outgoing and adventurous. This is especially relevant if your current circle of friends includes pessimists and negative thinkers whose attitudes can, unfortunately, be just as infectious as positivity.

I recommend you challenge yourself. Building up your self-confidence can also be a question of moving out of your comfort zone and trying something new and challenging. This can be any kind of goal, from learning a new language or skill to running your first marathon. This will give you a new focus in your life as well as possibly pushing you beyond what you thought were your limitations. Once you have risen to the challenge, you will be able to look back on it as being even more evidence that you are an accomplished, self-confident person who is capable of anything. Moving to a new job can also help. We spend around a third of our lives at work, so it's impossible to estimate just how important it is to build your self-worth. It is fine when we receive regular praise and know that we are doing our jobs well, but often it can feel like a distinctly undermining experience - for example if the work is unchallenging and repetitive.

The secret to building self-confidence at work is to either request a transfer to a role that you would find more satisfying or to move jobs altogether. Not only will the new role create a more stimulating atmosphere for you, but it is also certain to be a real confidence booster too.

Shape up and eat healthy. It is a fact that if we feel good about how we look, our confidence radiates out. That doesn't mean we need to have super model or film star looks; we just need to feel that we are making the absolute best of ourselves.

One of the most effective self-esteem exercises we can do is actual exercise. If this is also linked to a physical challenge that we have set ourselves that boost of confidence will help us to grow. It is also important to consider diet. If we feel that we are eating healthy and making all the right choices, it can give both a physical and a psychological boost to our self-esteem.

I would lastly recommend you take the philosophical approach. While all the suggestions given so far have focused on action and decisiveness, if you really want to know how to improve self-esteem then you will also need to be a little more thoughtful and philosophical.

Things won't always go your way and there is nothing you can do about that. The one thing you can control is how you react to these setbacks. Try to see them less as failures and more as learning experiences. Next time a similar situation occurs, you should have the confidence to cope with it more effectively. And that, in turn, will do wonders for your overall sense of self-worth.

"Never become a victim. Do not accept the definition of your life from what others tell you. Challenge yourself"

Forgive and forgive yourself

Forgive yourself. Forgive, forget, and file everything that has hurt you. Keep all the good memories and forget about the rest. Stop thinking about your past and reliving things that were already there. Live in the present which is the only thing you truly have. It would be better than all the time you are devoting to your past regretting things that have already happened. Dedicate time to your future. Build everything that comes your way and live the moment.

Give yourself a chance because as human beings we are meant to make mistakes. You must have the ability not only to forgive people, but to forgive yourself. Let me remind you that what happened to you was not in vain. You have learned an incredibly good lesson. You may be your worst judge. Stop judging yourself and understand yourself from a side of love and peace. Let the past be the past, learn from your experience and close that chapter. When you conclude the lesson you must learn, believe it and make sure it is real so you can move forward.

Forgiveness is often defined as a deliberate decision to let go of feelings of anger, resentment, and retribution toward someone who you believe has wronged you. While you may be quite generous in your ability to forgive others, you may be much harder on yourself. Everyone makes mistakes, but learning how to learn from these errors, let go, move on, and forgive yourself is important for mental health and well-being.

Self-forgiveness is not about letting yourself off the hook nor is it a sign of weakness. The act of forgiveness, whether you are forgiving yourself or someone who has wronged you, does not suggest that you are condoning the behavior. Forgiveness means that you accept the behavior, you accept what has happened, and you are willing to move past it and move on with your life without ruminating over past events that cannot be changed. One therapeutic approach to self-forgiveness suggests that four key actions can be helpful. Forgiving yourself is about more than just putting the past behind you and moving on. It is about accepting what has happened and showing compassion to yourself. Facing what you have done or what has happened is the first step toward self-forgiveness. It is also the hardest step. If you have been making excuses, rationalizing, or justifying your actions to make them seem acceptable, it is time to face up and accept what you have done. By taking responsibility and accepting that you have engaged in actions that have hurt others, you can avoid negative emotions, such as excessive regret and guilt.

I want you to open up and express remorse. As a result of taking responsibility, you may experience a range of negative feelings, including guilt and shame. When you have done something wrong, it is completely normal, even healthy, to feel guilty about it. These feelings of guilt and remorse can serve as a springboard to positive behavior change. While guilt implies that you are a good person who did something bad, shame makes you see yourself as a bad person. This can bring up feelings of worthlessness which, left unresolved, can lead to addiction, depression, and aggression. Understand that making mistakes that you feel guilty about does not make you a bad person or undermine your intrinsic value.

Making amends is an important part of forgiveness, even when the person you are forgiving is yourself. (Of course, it only works if you re apologizing sincerely and effectively.) Just as you might not forgive someone else until they have made it up to you in some way, forgiving yourself is more likely to stick when you feel like you have earned it. One way to move past your guilt is to take action to rectify your mistakes. Apologize if it is called for and look for ways that you can make it up to whomever you have hurt. It may seem as if this portion of the process benefits only the person you have harmed, but there is something in it for you as well. Fixing your mistake means you will never have to wonder if you could have done more.

I recommend you focus on renewal. Everyone makes mistakes and has things for which they feel sorry or regretful. Falling into the trap of rumination, self-hatred, or even pity can be damaging and make it difficult to maintain your self-esteem and motivation. Forgiving yourself often requires finding a way to learn from the experience and grow as a person. To do this, you need to understand why you behaved the way you did and why you feel guilty. What steps can you take to prevent the same behaviors again in the future? Yes, you might have messed up, but it was a learning experience that can help you make better choices in the future.

Limitation is important. While self-forgiveness is a powerful practice, it is important to recognize that this model is not intended for people who unfairly blame themselves for something they are not responsible for. People who have suffered abuse, trauma, or loss for example, may feel shame and guilt even though they had no control. This can be particularly true when people feel they should have been able to predict, and therefore avoid, a negative outcome (an example of what is known as the hindsight bias).

There are benefits to forgiveness. The standard axiom within psychology has been that forgiveness is a good thing and that it conveys several benefits, whether you have experienced a minor slight or have suffered a much more serious grievance. This includes both forgiving others as well as yourself. Letting go and offering yourself forgiveness can help boost your feelings of wellness and improve your image of yourself. Numerous studies have demonstrated that when people practice self-forgiveness, they experience lower levels of depression and anxiety. Similarly, self-compassion is associated with higher levels of success, productivity, focus, and concentration. I believe we back at square one. It all starts with you. Forgive yourself and forgive. Forget and file away.

"Every day is an opportunity to be someone better. Maybe today's your day!"

Life Lessons

Life is happening too quickly and unfortunately; we do not realize the value of it until we end up passing. It is constantly giving us lessons that we often do not understand why, but everything has a purpose. The five most important lessons you must learn are the following:

- Appreciate what you have. (We normally don't value the people we have closest to us.)
- Value who is real. (True friendship is not about who came first or who knows you the most. It's about who arrived and never left.)
- Take care of people. (If you don't take care of them in your present, don't expect to see them in the future because by then you will already be their past.)
- Family is not always bloodshed. (Family are the people who want to be in your life and want you in theirs. They accept you for who you are, and that is why blood is not the most important thing when we speak in love.)
- Do not miss opportunities. (In life there are three things that do not go back... The arrow throne, the uttered word, and the lost opportunity.)

Think about it. Value your life and live to the fullest. If you have made a mistake, start over. You now have the opportunity. Life's lessons are a beautiful gift, but they do not always come wrapped in a shiny red bow. Sometimes tragedy brings us wisdom. Sometimes joy does. Other times we stumble upon life-changing lessons when we least expect to.

No matter how they come to us, life's lessons are valuable and worth cherishing. Use them as a guide to live unapologetically without limits. To start fresh and move forward there are a lot of things you are going to want to drop. Whether it is a betrayal, bad childhood, divorce, or bad job, you must let it go and move forward.

You cannot do anything about what happened in the past, but you can do something about your future. Your past is not as important as what is ahead; you cannot let it poison your future. There is a lot the world can teach us.

I advise you to stop sharing your dreams with people who try to hold you back, even if it is your parents. If you are the kind of person who senses there is something out there for you beyond whatever it is you are expected to do, if you want to be EXTRA ordinary, you will not get there by hanging around a bunch of people who tell you that you are not extraordinary. Instead, you will probably become as ordinary as they expect you to be.

There are so many lessons I wish I had learned while I was young enough to appreciate and apply them. The thing with wisdom, and often with life lessons in general, is that they are learned in retrospect, long after we needed them. The good news is that other people can benefit from our experiences and the lessons we have learned.

"I don't know the secret to success, but the secret to failure is trying to please everybody." You do not need everyone to agree with you or even like you. Its human nature to want to belong, to be liked, respected, and valued, but not at the expense of your integrity and happiness. Other people cannot give you the validation you seek. That must come from inside. Speak up, stick to your guns, assert yourself when you need to, demand respect, stay true to your values. This is one of the life lessons you must learn to stop being a people pleaser.

In life we must also learn that your health is the most valuable asset. Health is a valuable treasure. Always appreciate, nurture, and protect it. Good health is often wasted in young people before they have a chance to appreciate it for what it is worth. We tend to take our good health for granted because it is just there. We do not have to worry about it, so we do not really pay attention to it until we have to. Heart disease, bone density, stroke, cancer. The list of preventable diseases is long, so take care of your health now or you will regret it later.

"Life is what happens while you're busy making other plans." No matter how carefully you plan and how hard you work, sometimes things just do not work out the way you want them to and that is okay. We have all these expectations; predetermined visions of what our "ideal" life will look like, but all too often, that is not the reality of the life we end up with. Sometimes our dreams fail and sometimes we just change our minds mid-course. Sometimes we must flop to find the right course and sometimes we just have to try a few things before we find the right direction.

But it is not all about you. You are not the epicenter of the universe. It is exceedingly difficult to view the world from a perspective outside of your own since we are always so focused on what is happening in our own lives. What do I have to do today? What will this mean for me? For my career, for my life? What do I want? It is normal to be intensely aware of everything that is going on in your own life, but you need to pay as much attention to what is happening around you. How things affect other people in the world as you do to your own life. It helps to keep things in perspective.

There is no shame in knowing. No one has it all figured out. Nobody has all the answers. There is no shame in saying "I don't know." Pretending to be perfect does not make you perfect. It just makes you neurotic to keep up the pretense of manufactured perfection.

We have this idea that there is stigma or shame in admitting our limitations or uncertainty, but we ca not possibly know everything. We all make mistakes and mess up occasionally. We learn as we go, that is life. Besides, nobody likes a know-it-all. A little vulnerability makes you human and oh so much more relatable.

Show LOVE. Love is more than a feeling, it's a CHOICE that burst of initial exhilaration. Pulse quickening love and passion does not last long. But that does not mean long-lasting love is not possible. Love is not just a feeling; it's a choice that you make every day. We must choose to let annoyances pass, to forgive, to be kind, to respect, to support, and to be faithful. Relationships take work. Sometimes it is easy and sometimes it is incredibly hard. It is up to us to choose how we want to act, think, and speak in a relationship as perspective is a beautiful thing. Typically, when we are worried or upset, it is because we have lost perspective.

Everything that is happening in our lives seems so big, so important, so do or die, but in the grand picture, this single hiccup often means next to nothing. The fight we are having, the job we did not get, the real or imagined slight, the unexpected need to shift course, the thing we wanted, but did not get. Most of it will not matter 20, 30, 40 years from now. It is hard to see long term when all you know is short term, but unless it is life-threatening, let it go and move on.

Do not take anything for granted. We often do not appreciate what we have until it is gone: that includes your health, your family and friends, your job, the money you have or think you will have tomorrow. When you are young, it seems that your parents will always be there, but they will not. You think you have plenty of time to get back in touch with your old friends or spend time with new ones, but you do not. You have the money to spend, or you think you will have it next month, but you might not.

Nothing in your life is not guaranteed to be there tomorrow, including those you love. This is a hard life lesson to learn, but it may be the most important of all: **Life can change in an instant.**

Make sure you appreciate what you have, while you still have it.

"Every saint has a past and every sinner has a future"

Your intuition

Albert Einstein said that "the intuitive mind is a gift and that the rational mind is a faithful servant". We have created a society in which we honor the servant and have forgotten the gift. In other words, we have stopped trusting our intuition and those famous hunches. We have a sixth sense for a reason, and one of the most important creators of the technological world taught us that. Steve Jobs, where he said, "you should listen to your own voice without letting anyone turn off that famous voice."

The most important thing is that you always follow your heart and your intuition because somehow, they already know who you will become. All the rest is secondary, so if the message comes to you, I hope you trust that hunch because you are right. Things do work in a certain way so listen to your sixth sense.

What is intuition really? Intuition is a "knowing" that cannot be explained by fact or thought, but through a deep inner feeling. It is those "I feel it in my gut" and "something doesn't feel quite right" moments and you cannot explain why. And my question is: **How often have you ignored that knowing little voice because it just did not make sense?**

Most of us do believe that our intuition, also known as our inner knowing voice, has value but we are at a complete loss as to how to access it and how to hear it. We are even more dumbfounded as to how to use it on demand. You only know it happened to you so many times and some of it was so obvious you smirked when you think back to what could have been avoided, **had you just paid a little more attention.**

"Intuition doesn't tell you what you want to hear; it tells you what you need to hear."

Intuition is a build-up of experiences, instincts, and senses, which includes heightening the touch, feeling, sight, hearing, and taste to its very peak. Intuition comes from the observation of one's own mental and emotional processes. It is more of "feel" rather than "logic". **It is your ability to sense things before they hit you.** For example, when you meet someone for the first time and shake hands, you may intuitively sense through touch and sight that you cannot trust this person. This could be an intense feeling because in your heart and gut you know that something is wrong. You may not know exactly why or have any logical reasoning for feeling that way, but at that very moment, you know that you must listen and trust that overwhelming feeling of danger.

On the contrary, it can also be a warm feeling of inner peace and love in your heart, because you know that everything is going to be okay. Although we receive messages in different ways, we all receive them, even if we are not tapping into them. Some of us feel things, while others see or hear them.

"Intuition is the supra-logic that cuts out all the routine processes of thought and leaps straight from the problem to the answer."
-Robert Graves

From my own experience, I have often mistaken my intuition for fear. It can be confusing, and it is important to know the difference. After all, I do not want you to pass up your perfect opportunity out of fear because you have mistakenly felt there was an intuitive warning keeping you from moving in that direction.

Intuition can be recognized as an inner guidance, a kind of knowing, or you might say an internal compass. We use terms like "hunch", "a gut feeling", "just a feeling", and "instinct" to describe the way intuition influences our behavior. **Intuition lead towards a path that makes us feel comfortable, even if we are not certain.**

Fear or negative emotion on the other hand, can express itself through a physical response such as aggressiveness, sweating, an adrenaline rush, or a racing heart. Fear may cause us to run away and hide and avoid and dictates a decision that makes us feel relieved as though we just survived a threat to our very existence. Do not get me wrong, a sudden rush of intuition may be felt strongly as fear and certainly should be looked at. But understanding the difference is important if we really want to properly access our intuition.

Try not to use your intuition if you are using your head too much because then you will be using your ego and your intuition will not be able to come through. Usually, this is a place of fear, so it is not a good time as you will be too reactive. Instead, use your intuition when you are calm, not rushed and have time to think things over.

"A quiet mind is able to hear intuition over fear."

I recommend you improve access to your intuition. Before you can improve access to your intuition, you must first be able to hear it within the noise of your busy life. **You need to slow down and listen**, which often requires solitude. It would greatly help by taking some time away from your everyday busyness. Even something as brief as going for a walk to turn up the volume of your intuition.

Here are three methods I believe are the most effective to improve access to your intuition:

1. Practice Mindfulness

   Mindfulness means to focus on being in the moment. It is a great technique to filter out all the distractions in your environment and your brain. When you do that, you can hear your intuition loud and clear.

2. Trust Your Gut

   Research has shown that emotion and intuition have a physical presence in our gut. The gut is lined with a network of neurons and it is often referred to as the "*second brain*". It is known as the enteric nervous system (ENS) and it contains around 100 million neurons, which is more than the spinal cord and peripheral nervous system (PNS) but less than the brain. This is the reason why we get "sick" about having to make a tough decision or knowing we have made a bad one. Your trusty gut is not only essential in a tense situation, but also your everyday coach. Many of us have forgotten how to listen to our intuition and trust our gut.

3. Use Your Dream Time Well

   When we dream, our brain processes information that is left over from the day. Dreams are packed with valuable information such as learnings, experiences, and memories. Paying attention to our dreams can provide information that we may not have access when we are awake. Therefore, before going to sleep, it is essential for you to direct your thoughts to any unresolved issues and think about possible options or solutions as you are falling asleep. Close your eyes and let your brain do the rest.

"Pay attention to your dreams. They could be telling you things that you need to know."

Do me a favor and from this point on enjoy your intuition. The main reason that some people are more intuitive than others is that they listen to their intuition instead of ignoring or doubting it. Many people from today's society have this crazy idea that being intuitive means to ignore their analytical mind and their critical thinking skills. But it is not. There is a difference between using reason as a system of checks and using it to go against what your intuition knows to be true.

Let us learn to honor and enjoy the wisdom of our forgotten gift.

"The intuitive mind is a sacred gift, and the rational mind is a faithful servant. We have created a society that honors the servant and has forgotten the gift."
— Albert Einstein

Confidence

Confidence is beautiful no matter your size, no matter your weight. Be confident in who you are, and you will be beautiful. Your skin is not paper, so do not cut it. Your face is not a mask, so do not cover it. Your size is not a book, so do not judge it. Your life is not a film, so do not end it. You are beautiful. Beauty has nothing to do with looks. It is all about how you are as a person and how you make others feel about themselves.

You are beautiful no matter what anyone would say. Words cannot bring you down. A beautiful face does not mean anything without a beautiful heart. You are imperfect and inevitably flawed yet you are BEAUTIFUL. When I tell you that you are beautiful, I do not just mean your appearance. I mean all of you. I do not need to know you to know you are beautiful. If you do not know you are beautiful knowing yourself, then we are lacking a great deal of confidence.

Confidence is a belief in oneself, the conviction that one could meet life's challenges to succeed and the willingness to act accordingly. Being confident requires a realistic sense of one's capabilities and feeling secure in that knowledge. Projecting confidence helps people gain credibility, make a strong first impression, deal with pressure, and tackle personal and professional challenges. It is also an attractive trait, as confidence helps put others at ease. Confidence is not an innate, fixed characteristic. It is an ability that can be acquired and improved over time. Social confidence can be developed by practicing in social settings. Individuals can observe the structure and flow of any conversation before jumping in, and they can prepare questions or topics to discuss ahead of time.

Anxiety can take hold when people are plagued by self-doubt. Putting themselves in and getting accustomed to the specific situation they **fear** can assure people that nothing truly bad will happen. The activity gets easier with practice.

Outside of a social context, one can gain a sense of confidence from personal and professional accomplishments. Continuing to set and meet goals can enable the belief that one is competent and capable. Being confident means knowing that you can handle the emotional outcome of whatever you will face. Begin by acknowledging every emotion. Including difficult emotions rather than avoiding them. Speaking up for yourself, limiting self-criticism and other strategies can help build emotional strength and confidence.

People often receive conflicting information about how to achieve self-confidence. Confidence seems to have an amorphous quality, which makes the concept difficult to grasp and even more challenging to teach. But rest assured it can be done. Developing confidence is learnable and actionable. Confidence develops when you have a deep sense that you can handle the emotional outcome of whatever you face or pursue. Another way to put it is that confidence is the felt sense of a "can-do" attitude.

Throughout my years working with patients, teaching and now with my clients, I have identified six ways that people build confidence, and five of them can be practiced daily. Trusting that you are emotionally strong is the foundation, followed by speaking, taking action, ending self-criticism, and absorbing compliments.

1. The first step is to allow yourself to be aware of experience and move through the full range of your feelings, both pleasant and unpleasant. Most of us do well with pleasant

feelings but can be distracted by unpleasant ones. The key here is that you are choosing awareness, or "knowing what you know," as opposed to avoidance and "trying not to know what you know." In this case, it means dealing with eight unpleasant feelings: sadness, shame, helplessness, anger, vulnerability, embarrassment, disappointment, and frustration. Allowing yourself to move toward pain and deal with the feelings that result from disappointment builds emotional strength. When you choose to be aware of and in touch with the full range of what you experience, it is very centering, grounding, and peaceful. You feel truer to yourself. This is the start of building confidence.

2. The second step is speaking up or expressing yourself with discretion and in a positive, kind, and well-intentioned manner by telling the truth about what you experience. It is saying what you need to say with whom you wish to speak; at the time you need. Think about how frequently a therapist or person close to you tells you to speak up. There is a good reason why they advise you to do so. When you tell your well-intended truth, you will find that speaking up gives your confidence a major boost because it helps you live more authentically.

3. The third step is to take actions that move you toward your **goals** even if it seems hard to take those risks. With both speaking up and taking action, it is not that you have confidence and then speak or do something positive; instead, it is through speaking and taking action that you develop confidence.

4. The fourth is to end harsh self-criticism or negative **self-talk.** This behavior not only fosters doubt but can rob you of the will to pursue your goals. Despite some people's beliefs that being mean to yourself helps motivate you, hurting yourself with thoughts and words is profoundly

damaging. When you are tempted to belittle yourself, use your awareness of this temptation as a signal that something harder to know or bear is trying to make itself known to you. Then ask yourself: Why is it difficult for me to know or bear? Any insights that emerge can help guide your future actions.

5. Though many of us are inclined to dismiss them, the fifth step is to accept the genuine compliments you receive. Compliments act as a mirror and reflection of yourself. As you let yourself take them in, they can help you settle into yourself, perhaps allowing you to see that you are already the person you want to become.

These actions can increase your confidence – the deep sense that you can handle the emotional outcome of whatever you face or want to pursue.

"People who have trust issues just need to look in the mirror. There they will meet the person who betrayed them the most."
-Shannon L. Alder

Bullied

For those who had a rough time as a child. For those who are or were bullied. There are better people in the world, do not let the worst do the worst to you. You deserve the best in life. Sometimes, all you need is for someone to just be there. If you do not have that special someone create your own and even if they cannot solve your problems, just knowing there is someone there who cares can make all the difference.

I am going to level with you. I hate bullying and I will do everything I possibly can to prevent it from being a common occurrence. People share my view on this topic and believe it should be one of the main priorities to monitor. I did not start believing what I do because everyone else did or because I witnessed it happen. I experienced it; I was a victim. I want to talk to you about bullying, its effects, and some of my story. Hopefully, it will leave you with a little more insight of me and a little more insight as to what bullying is and how to prevent it.

Picture a little girl with beautiful height, gorgeous smile, great complexion, and a bag waddling down to these massive school gates. She was full of anticipation, wonder, happiness, excitement, motivation, and courage. She seems like a little girl with an extremely bright future, doesn't she? Little did she know she would not stay that way for awfully long. From the minute she walked into those gates, from the minute she spoke to the first person she was instantly targeted, and she did not know why. She did not ask for it and she did not do anything to deserve it. She became the center of every fight, and every hateful word. She was told she was worthless. She was told she was fat, ugly, annoying, stupid, and too tall to even fit in. She was told she did not belong in this world. She was told she should end her life. She was told she was nothing. She was told that she should not try because she was a failure, and she could never achieve anything. This girl was 11 years old. Yet these words and actions left a very distinct imprint in her mind for years. That girl is 36 now. That girl was me.

It started in elementary school. Jane S. Roberts, my elementary school and it continued all the way up to high school. Until eventually it became too much. So unbearable that I started acting dumb, as if I would not understand nothing in school just to get out and go for my GED. Unfortunately, it did not stop there either, it continued through the rest of those years. That was my entire elementary school life. How do you guys remember your last day of school? Probably crying because you will miss everyone and laughing back at all the memories. I spent my last school year in the bathrooms, sitting in the stalls eating my lunch because I felt too threated. Too ashamed to walk outside those doors and face the harsh words people had to say.

In what sick and cruel world are kids belittled to the point that they go to the effort to hide? They must go to the great length of hiding and making an effort not to be seen because they are so scared in their own environment? These people, they did not know how much they were hurting me, how much they were affecting me. Bullies do not understand that what they say DOES hurt that person weather they show it or not. How could you possibly tell what that person is feeling or what that person is going through? You do not know everything. It takes a certain level of humility to say; "I actually don't like that, it's killing me." I had not a single shred of confidence.

I have spent the past three years rebuilding my confidence back up again. After what I went through, I did not believe in myself anymore. I thought I was worthless, and I started to believe what those people were saying about me and that is when it starts. When you start to believe what they say, that is when depression, anxiety, and that self-hate starts. It is proven that the more you are told something the more you start to believe it. These kids are targeted every day, which is 365 days a year that these kids are forced to get up and face this cruelty. That is incredible! The amount of sheer determination they must adapt to every single day just to get through it.

I want you to know that this is not something to play around with. Check out how serious this is. I assure you that 98% of you (not excluding myself) have teased someone in your life. What if the person you are teasing is the person who is thinking of committing suicide? People think that bullying is tough, it is not tough. You want to know what tough is? Go up to someone you tease and say you are sorry. Or go up to someone that teases you and say please stop. That is tough! What number of suicides must take place before society realizes that bullying kills people? How do we get through to people that are pulling others down? It is not funny, and it is not a game.

Luckily, I am thankful to have my support system. I learned that I have people there for me who care for me and will bring me back from that edge.

Because of the people who I call my friends and family I am still here. Because I have my children I am still here. We, as a community, need to be that support network for these kids and these students who cannot speak for themselves. We need to be the change. Bullying happens way more than it should, but you always have the power to make a difference. If someone is alone at your hangout spot, will you offer to be his friend? If someone gets pushed down, will you lift them back up? If a friend is sad because of a mean text or message, will you send some kind words to make them smile? If someone puts you down, will you believe them or choose to believe in yourself?

Please be careful with words you say to others. What we think is funny or cool could end up being powerfully hurtful. It takes ten times as long to pull yourself together as it does to fall apart. I hope people that have been considered bullies are reading this and realize how much pain you inflicted on people around you. To those who have been a victim and fallen into depression, you can get through this. I promise that things will get better. They did for me and they can for you. Do not hesitate to stand up for yourself and what you believe in. If we unite, we can stop the increasing level of bullying. We can help all generations get better and teach the world to be kind to each other. To respect each other for who they are.

The end of bullying starts with you. Remember there is always someone out there who loves you and will love you with all your flaws and problems you have gone through. If you are depressed, do not hide it. Find someone you trust, let them know and let them help you. (It's a thing- Do it!) Showing emotions does not mean you are weak. It means you are human. Do not change who you are for anyone.

Be a part of the positive not the negative. Speak up and spread kindness.

"Never be intimidated by your challenges. No matter how hard they are, they will bow to your destiny."

My choice is to be happy, what is yours?

"It feels like nothing makes sense"

-What doesn't make sense?

"Life and just things, I can care less to be dead or alive"

- But why? If you are here.

"I haven't been here for a while. I lie to everyone acting like everything is ok but..."

-But what?

"I'm not happy. Nothing gives me enthusiasm; nothing makes me feel good. I'm tired, I'm sleepy. I can sleep more than 16 hours and I still feel tired"

-Do you know why?

"If I knew why I wouldn't be here"

-You have grown tied to the past, instead of forgiving and being understanding with yourself. You are filling yourself with negative thoughts and fear. So, change your thoughts!

"But no matter how much I try they're always there"

-That is the choice you made. You are your own victim. Only when you learn to control your own thoughts that is when your life will change. So long, goodbye!

"Nooo, don't leave! Help me!"

-I would love to but only you can make that choice.

~" To love is to find your happiness in others happiness."

Sick of being sick

The other day I was walking down the street asking myself the same thing repeatedly. How can I be happy? Reality is that I am so sick of being sick that I am not happy. Where is happiness? How can I find it? Why have I not found it yet? Suddenly I saw it. It was right there in front of me. Happiness is like a butterfly. The more you chase it, the more elusive it becomes. If you pay attention to other things, then it will come sit on your shoulder when you least expect it. That is why I want you to pay close attention to the story.

There once was a man who dedicated his life to finding happiness through money. When he reached the end of his life, he went to collect his retirement fund. This retirement fund was assured, no one could take it away from him. That same night he got the news that he was dying. What use did his money have now? Where did he leave happiness? No happiness and no peace. Sure, many of you will say he was happy in his own way. But if you have been up and down and have met all types of people, we know that happiness is not accomplished while searching for it.

Do you want to know how happiness is accomplished? Do you want me to reveal the secret? It's simple. Happiness is reached when you stop looking for it. When you realize that you still have oxygen to breathe you discover it was always around. Happiness was always there. When you leave aside your ego and your constant search for happiness you will then notice what is important in life.

Yes, I have health issues. Yes, I have difficulties doing what a regular person without health issues can do. But all I hear myself saying now is I HAVE. Sitting in the hospital being witness to what someone else lost made me realize how happy I have always been. We are not playing a board game, meaning we only have one life so let's live it to the max. Those that do not have much, never complain and move on with hope instead of complaints. Whenever you feel down or unhappy read back on this passage and gain courage to keep going. You got this!

~You do not know how strong you are until being strong is the only option you have left.
-Therapy in Sessions

You can do anything

I have always said to myself, what can't I do? I always grew up believing that I can do anything. That I can accomplish anything because of everything that I saw in my household. Not everybody turns out good you know, and it is not always your fault either. I need you to stop blaming yourself for things that you had no control over.

I had a great childhood, but my parents never believed in my dreams. That does not make them bad parents, it just means they had another focus. Some children are raised in the worst conditions and yet turned out to be the most respectful people in life. While some are raised with everything such as both parents, the best education, good wealth, yet turn out to be the worst. Unbelievably it may not be the parent's fault.

The point here is that you are what you say you are. You must believe in yourself disregarding what anyone says or thinks about you. That includes family and friends. Education is required I know, but even without it people have made it very far in life because they had that one thing they truly needed within them to be capable of anything. A goal! My parents did not catch my dreams. Oh well, they are not a dreamcatcher anyhow. That does not mean I cannot accomplish them. My parents had a task until I turned a certain age. At this point I am my own responsibility. What's up with you? Come on, get up and go for it! You do not need money, a car, or anybody to believe in you. All you need is YOU to believe in you.

If you want a girlfriend, ask her out! If you want a man, ask him out! If they are with someone just wait. If you have the patience and it is meant to be for you, they will breakup. If they do not breakup, then go to the next candidate. (You will be ok. It was not meant to be) we don't always make the best choices you know. If you want money, get it! I mean, we all must work for it. If you do not have a car, go walking, or in a bike, or however but do it. You will love the outcome.

My car caught on fire on my birthday two years ago, so I have no car. My cell phone is continuously disconnected. I am a single mother of two. I live day by day and I love it. You will enjoy going through your obstacles as well if you believe in yourself. Trust me! If you want a specific job, simply apply for it. If they are not hiring, go back again and again until they are. Believe that they will hire you as in between the process something better will appear. That is simply how it works and how it always happens. Bottom line is you are capable of anything. Believe in yourself like I believe in me that is why I stand today. I'm a living proof.

Repeat these words aloud: *I am capable of doing anything I want to do!* Who speaks to their instincts, speaks to the deepest secrets of mankind and finds the radiated response.

"For those who believe, no proof is necessary. For those who don't believe, no proof is possible. Keep life moving forward, looking backwards is only for time travelers."

Brown skin girls

The most common way people give up power is by thinking they do not have any. Success is liking yourself, liking what you do, and liking how you do it. I was built this way for a reason, so I am going to use it. I am a feminist, and what that means to me is much the same as the meaning that I am black. It means that I must undertake to love myself and respect myself as though my very life depends upon self-love and self-respect. One of the lessons that I grew up with was that you must always stay true to yourself and never let what somebody else says distract you from your goals.

Caring for myself is not self-indulgence, its self-preservation. If we give our children sound self-love, they will be able to deal with whatever life puts before them. I need to see my own beauty and continue to be reminded that I am enough. That I am worthy of love without effort, that I am beautiful. That the texture of my hair, the size of my lips, the color of my skin and the feelings that I have are all worthy and ok. We have so much coming in as sisters that I ask, when has our interior light ever been put at the forefront?

We constantly want to give to people, but too much not caring for yourself is not a good thing. Self-care is a priority, and we must do it more. Don't ever let anyone talk about your skin color, and if they do it is only because you shine bright like a diamond. Because of the beautiful color you carry when you are in a room, they notice you. It is a beautiful thing. Even if it makes others uncomfortable, I will always love who I am and so should you. Let me remind you that without black, no color has depth.

"Brown skin.

Ref: Everything beautiful, cute and good."

How you need to start your day

The remarkable thing about life is that we have a choice every day regarding the attitude we will embrace for that day. We cannot change our past. We cannot change the fact that people act a certain way. We cannot change the inevitable. The only thing we can do is play with the one thing we have and that is our attitude. I am challenging you to make the most out of this battle. Live it like it could be your last. Do not spend it negative and defeated. Enjoy today and no matter how bad things could be in your life, there is always something you can be thankful for. Doctors and psychologists have proven that the attitude you have for the day is set the first eight minutes. Do you want to be sad, depressed, mad, or do you want to be grateful? I will encourage you to do it just for today. Do an experiment and really be grateful for many parts of you. Grateful for where you are right now in your life. Here you are. You are learning. You are progressing.

Do mirror work. Mirror work is so powerful. Talk to yourself in the mirror, not to hurt yourself, but to love yourself. You have the power. You can think yourself into a good mood, or you could think yourself into a bad mood. You can think that you have the worst life of the planet, or you can purposely look around and see how blessed you are. Count all the things that God has done for you. Notice how you can get happy and grateful suddenly. What you think is up to you. I say this all the time, happiness is a choice. You are as happy as you choose to be. If you are unhappy is because you are choosing to be unhappy. Do not blame your husband, your wife, your children, or anybody else. It is a choice.

If you have the right attitude you can enjoy anything you do. You can enjoy mowing the lawn. You can enjoy the driving world. You can enjoy cleaning the house. You do not have to enjoy part of your life and dwell on the other part. You can decide and enjoy everything you do. From sunup to sundown I guarantee it. Every single day of your life is a new day. If you want to improve a bad day, have a big dream. I do not mean go to sleep, have a nap, and have that kind a dream. I mean see something beyond where you are right now. Have hope. Have an expectancy. Believe that things are going to change. Believe that things will get better. Learn to smile. Learn to laugh. Enjoy the simple things in life. Enjoy where you are in life today. If you let yourself get negative, bitter, and depressed, that does not make matters worse. It just draws in more negativity so as hard as it is sometimes, it goes against human nature. You have got to get up in the morning when things are not going your way and just find something to be grateful for.

If we are speaking bad things, negative things, downgrading things, critical and judgmental things, we are eating those words and they are going to fall inside of us and make us unhappy. If we talk about good things, thankful things, and how much we appreciate what God has done for us, it just makes us happy. You can think yourself into a bad mood, or you can think yourself into a good mood. You can also talk yourself into a bad or a good mood. We may not be able to help how we feel, but we can control what we do.

I suggest that we talk in the mirror a lot. First thing in the morning when you get up go look in the mirror and just say I love you. Start to connect with yourself. Forgive yourself from the mirror. Talk to yourself. I give myself permission to be great. I give myself permission to live in joy. I am happy, successful, and prosperous.

Please give it a try and tell your story.

~Get up, I will give you a new chance to live.

-Therapy in Sessions

Your peace is not negotiable

I will not allow you to alter my peace. I do not chase you to know where you are going. I can know everything without having to move from here. I do not need to check your phone to know you are talking to another woman. I do not need to touch anything of yours to know what you are doing. With only observing you is enough. I am very calm because nothing or no one is going to disturb my peace. My peace is not negotiable, much less my serenity. You once told me I was never going to find someone like you and that is the idea.

I guess it is true what they say about getting older and becoming wiser. This year I turned 36 and it was the year I realized the importance of protecting and maintaining my peace. This year I decided that my peace is non-negotiable, and if you threaten that, no matter who you are, a shift will have to take place. Period!

Growing up as religious, I was constantly taught to forgive, and most times that was as far as it went. Just forgive them, turn the other cheek, and then (hope to) forget. Now that I am older though, I learned that when someone constantly threatens my tranquility, I should forgive them, yes, but it does not stop there. I can forgive them, and then I can let them go.
Honestly, I was taught that cutting people out of your life is an ungodly thing to do. That it has something to do with holding a grudge or keeping malice. Recently I learned that removing people from your space is one of the wisest things you can do (when done right) to protect your peace. Why should you be around something or

someone that continues to come up against you? (Spoiler Alert: You shouldn't!).

If your life is overfilled, you may need to set some limits. Stop doing some of the least important things, the things that honestly do not matter that much. Set a limit for how many times you will check inboxes, Instagram, Twitter etc. per day. Say no if you really do not have the time or just do not want to. Do what work for you? Long walks, music, yoga, meditation or going for a swim? Find out and do that.

Unclutter your world, unclutter your mind. Just take three minutes to declutter your circle; weather if it is your group of friends or family, workspace, or the room you are in. An uncluttered, simplified and ordered space around you brings clarity and order to the mind. Do not stop there. Declutter, simplify, and organize your home and life too to live in a more relaxing environment. Now is now. But if something negative from the past – something someone said, something someone did is still on your mind then accept and let that feeling and thought in instead of trying to push it away.

When you accept that, it is then it starts to lose power. While the facts may still be there in your head the negative feelings become a lot less powerful. At this point, let that thing go like you are throwing out a bag of old clothes. Direct your focus to the present moment and something better instead.
I would like you to remember these five little words that'll help you to stay sane: *ONE THING AT A TIME*. By keeping those words in mind and letting them guide you through your day you will be less stressed and more focused. That will not only bring more inner peace but also help you do a better and quicker job at pretty much anything.

"Whatever does not bring calm and serenity to your life, leave it behind. There is nothing more valuable than losing your peace."

You don't have to wait so long when you know what's right

Personally, I do not play around with marriage specially if there are children involved. One thing I notice is that some couples are blinded by the red flags that come up within the first year of them getting together. We all see the red flags that tell us that is not going to work. But we ignore them for ambitious purposes. That is real. Sometimes it is best to nip it in the butt before things get worse.

I am a woman. To me, it is worse for us because of that women intuition. We know if it is going to work or not. As human beings some of us are loyal as heck and due to that loyalty, we choose not to break some things up. Why? Because you swore for better or for worse? The part that you got confused in is that there must be love in it. Real love. Trust. Many of you are willing to stay with someone that betrayed your trust all because of fear. You are so terrified that you are willing to accept being treated less than you are.

You are not alone. What happens is that we have convinced ourselves that being disrespected is better than being alone. You have the power. There is power in rediscovering your own voice. Why wait so long to free yourself? Why has your husband, wife, or children been living a fake reality of happiness? That does not work anymore.

The love of today is a contract. It should not be. Such is life. Now a days we look for what a person has to offer. We look for physical, race, culture. Whatever happened with feelings, connection, and chemistry? Now a day's women in good standings get approached by the cashier male at Publix and they quickly look away. Without even knowing that that man could possibly have made her the happiest woman ever. Now a day's men are just living off women. Like, it's a thing!

The point is that you know what it is. You know if it is not going to work out. Staying around is not going to make anything any better. What you think is going good now will turn out sour. Maybe not now but in 20 years you will still regret it. Think ahead. Space is also a key to happiness. If you choose to stay in it then never stop dating. Have you not heard about the truth behind what you don't know what you have until it's gone? Why do we often take for granted the very things that deserve our gratitude the most? We do this with both people and possessions. The problem is many people do not realize this until the situation has come and passed. We take things for granted daily, always with the assumption that whenever we need something, it will be there.

There are many things we fail to realize the true value of until they are missing from our lives. Think of technology, the Internet, and your cell phone. You do not realize how vital your cell phone is to your life until you go days without it. Enjoy the little things in life because someday you will realize they were the big things.

This is a common thing once a relationship reaches its conclusion. When you become complacent with your partner, it is easy to fall into this trap. Happiness does not come as a result of getting what you do not have, rather it is recognizing and appreciating what you do have. If someone once made you happy, there is a great chance they still will. Think about it, maybe you are bored with your familiar routine, but that does not mean you should get rid of it. Do not lose something you have for something you think you want.

When people break up, it is common to regret it. You end the relationship because you think you can do better, but once you are out there in the dating world, you realize you had something amazing. Sometimes it is too little too late and you must learn from your unfortunate decision. What screws a person up is trying to live up to the image they create in their minds. There is no such thing as perfect, only perfect for you.

All I am saying is to appreciate what you have before it becomes what you had. What you have now was once everything you strove to attain. Just because something becomes repetitive does not mean it needs to be replaced. Think of how lucky you are to have someone you can be completely comfortable around. That is a true gift and one that should always be cherished. Appreciate all the things you have in life because you never know when that time will end. Clear the clutter inside your mind and realize what you have right now. Don't wait until you have lost it to finally see how much you took it for granted. Don't wait until you realize that without it, your foundation to make it through each day begins to crumble.

There is always someone else happier with less than what you have. Too many times people do not realize what they have because they are out looking for something better. The problem is that when they do realize it, they will come crawling back. Everyone falls into the trap that the grass is always greener on the other side. People make mistakes, it is part of human nature. If you really love this person, it may be in both people's best interest to give him or her another chance. Sometimes space makes people appreciate things they once had. You need to make it clear that you forgive one time, and one time only, and if this is what you genuinely want.

On the flip side, you can only want something when you have not got it. If you had it back, you would only get fed up with all the bad bits again and start wondering why you wanted it back in the first place. When you lose someone, you tend to remember the good parts. When you are with them, you tend to notice the bad parts; this is of course until you find the one you were truly meant to be with, and then the bad bits just seem endearing.

Do not take things for granted because they might not be there tomorrow. The thing is, very few people can see the impact of what they do now and how it relates to their futures. Which would you rather regret?: The present, where you have no idea what is happening as it is in real time and you have not the slightest conception of long-term consequences, or the past, where you can take your time to see things as they were? People make mistakes and leave the things they love most. They fail to appreciate the good thing they once had and as a result will continuously regret their decision.

People constantly want something more, something new, but sometimes the most valuable things are always what have been with us. Just because something is not happening for you right now does not mean that it never will. Happiness will never come to those who fail to appreciate what they already have. Just like you do not know what you have until it is gone. You do not know what you have been missing until it arrives.

"We are not responsible for emotions, but for what we do with the emotions."-Jorge Bugay

Never stop dating

Never stop dating. Not even if you are married. A lot of relationships fail because they become boring. Either one or the other becomes comfortable. If you want your relationship to last with passion you cannot be lazy because then how do you show love and expect someone to feel?

People get used to the person they met when you were on another level. They want to feel just that. They do not want that to end. Do not become someone different than who they fell in love with. You cannot lose that hunger to please. You must keep reminding them repeatedly the reasons why they fell in love you. They should never have to question their value in your life.

Stay in the audition mode. I am telling you not to ever stop dating even after marriage. Why? I need you to be "in audition mode"! When you are dating, what happens? You do everything you can. You go above and beyond just to please that person, just to impress them. Just to get that person's love. So, when you get it please do not change on them. Your partner wants to feel wanted, like you made them feel back then. They want to feel desired, like you made them feel back then. Your partner wants to feel respected, like you made them feel back then. It is on you to keep it passionate, spontaneous, and exciting. You always hear people say," I don't even know this person anymore". You need to take pride in not becoming a stranger to the person that fell in love with you. Remember the reason why you fell in love with them. Do not let any distractions make you forget that. Be awesome together. Have fun together. Do crazy things together. That is what life is about. Focus on the things that matter. What matters most is to give love to the people who love you.

After years in a long-term relationship, it is easy to slip into a complacent routine that is a little too comfortable. After all, sharing a toothbrush is not so sexy, and the silence you experience while the two of you are reading in bed might linger a little too long because you have maintained a casual text conversation all day.

It is inevitable that the surprises are not always present when you realize that your significant other has also become your best friend after spending so much time together over weeks and months and years. I suggests that people should be willing to "date themselves" - that is, treat themselves and be comfortable in solitude before committing to sharing time and even a life with someone else. While this lesson is clearly valuable, it can also be extended to those individuals already in a relationship. Whether you think you and your significant other are in a rut, or whether you simply know the importance of there always being so much more to learn about each other, dating your significant other is equally important in maintaining a healthy and lasting relationship.

Making time for weekly (or even simply bi-monthly) "date nights" may seem like an added stressor when two people are already pressed for time, but allotting a meal, an activity or simply an hour for a couple to reconnect can have some seriously therapeutic effects. Not just on the relationship, but on yourself. It is important to have that time as a couple to connect, relax and just enjoy each other's company. It may sound overly simple, but "dating," even while in a relationship, will remind you why you kept seeing this individual in the first place.

Getting out of the comfort zone of your apartments and dressing up in something other than PJs will serve as a reminder of the perhaps slightly-more-exciting people you guys were before becoming mutually exclusive. When you get super comfortable with another human being that is something to be celebrated, so why not make it a habit to take your love out for nights on the town? Showing the other person off will make you profoundly grateful to be in each other's company.

Sit in front of the TV and watch Netflix all day with your significant other, chances are the conversation will not vary much further than "pass the remote", or "that was a good movie." But out in public, you two might be encouraged to veer into the more interesting and sincere topics of that good debate. Being across a table from each other can help sustain a back-and-forth that is not only interesting and intellectually stimulating but can help you learn an additional something about one another.

It will definitely give you something to talk about. Your pillow talk does not have to be limited to the requisite: "How was your day?" "Fine." Going on dates will give you two more to reflect on, more to talk about, more inside jokes to serve as fodder that further alienates your friends.

It is easy to get caught up in the day-to-day, or perhaps even more technical aspects of your relationship. Like looking after a shared space, or your children. But going out of your typical routine and experiencing new things together will shake all that up, by ensuring that the two of you continue to make memories that do not simply involve cuddling solo on the couch. Scheduled dates can sustain a long-term relationship. They can serve as a reminder that you can still have fun with one another and share in how much the two of you enjoy occasionally getting out of the house.

"Love always that life takes care of giving you back what you give."

Why it is important to give back

Everything a human being does for themselves is taken to the grave the day of our departure. On the other hand, everything a human does for others they leave behind.

You want to begin to look and start developing generational thinking. What is it that I can leave for generations yet on board? All of us have the capacity to manifest greatness and participate in this game called life and to contribute. All of us have the responsibility to give something back because someone paid a price for us to be here. As we begin to look towards the future, we must ask ourselves the question, what kind of legacy do I want to leave? What kind of contribution do I want to leave in terms of the planet? How is it that we can give something today that will make a difference tomorrow?

Think about it, what talent do you have right now? What skill? The fact that you are still breathing means you are not through yet. Your business on earth is not completed yet. You have something to give, all of us do. We have in our hand's talent, skills, ability, and a conscience to make a tremendous difference in life. We do not even know it.

I want you to see yourself doing more, what is it that you would like to do right now? If you die today these are the things that will be said that you helped to create in making a better world. Somebody has made a sacrifice. Somebody has contributed. Somebody has given us a heads up. Somebody was there for us when we needed it. None of us make it by ourselves. Believe me, it is a fact.

What cause can you be involved in? How is it that you can give something back? I believe that when you have faced real difficulties and challenges in life that is when you can really appreciate giving back. That is when you can really appreciate sharing who you are because it gives your life a special kind of power. I believe that the people that make the greatest difference in life are the people that are givers. I have seen people who do not have, who cannot even afford to give and gave what they had. They did what they could. We can always give excuses or justification for not giving our best. Right now, when we begin to look at the conditions that exist in society, now more than ever we need people, both men and women to step forward and take a stand to make a difference.

I want you to ask yourself, what do I stand for? What kind of stand can I take with my life right now that would make a tremendous difference? I believe that the reason that most people go through life being spectators and takers as opposed to givers is because they have a limited vision of themselves. They cannot see themselves making a difference. It really does not matter how huge the problem is. It does not matter how disastrous things appear to be. Human beings have the capacity to take the most disastrous circumstances and make something positive, powerful, and meaningful out of it. Look at your life right now and ask yourself "how is it that I can give something back?" What do I stand for? What is the philosophy of my life? What do I honestly believe in? What belief I am I willing to give up my life for?

Find something that gives your life meaning. We live in a great country that enables us to contribute. Enables us to make a difference. We are here and experiencing a great deal of benefits because somebody at some point in time made a supreme sacrifice. All of us have a responsibility and obligation to give something back. Think about what you can be an asset to. Who is it that you can help? What good can you contribute? How is it that you have been holding back on yourself and on life? You showed up to do something. You are no accident. You have something to give. Just find some cause that you can begin to take a stand in. What is it that you are giving back? What kind of gift are you creating now?

"Solidarity is not about giving for charity, but worrying about common interests, and so no one is left behind."

It's not like you care anyway

Only those who genuinely care about you can hear you when you are quiet. Understanding is deeper than knowledge. There are many people who know you, but there are very few who understand you. The moment you start to wonder if you deserve better. YOU DO!

I have a confidence about my life that comes from standing tall on my own two feet. I cannot begin to tell you what you should do. Our life is an endless series of choices, and we decide who we are through those choices. For me, I accept the fact that not everyone will even like me, let alone care about me. I decided long ago that I do not care at all what someone's opinion of me personally may be. By this I mean that I do not allow anyone's opinion to touch me on an emotional level, so it does not affect my wellbeing or happiness.

I will listen intently to their opinions, especially the negative ones, but do it from a detached perspective. Like I was in a lecture in school. There may well be something they say that is worth giving thought to. After all, we all have aspects of ourselves that we are too close to see. Things that could be a way to improve who we are.

It is not difficult to not care about a judgmental person's opinion, yet to still care about them as a person. I still wish them well, and do not wish them any ill will. I tend to believe that they already have enough to overcome, and likely are not incredibly happy with themselves, so they judge the value and behaviors of others instead of their own. I feel sad for these people, but not sorry for them. They have chosen to be as they are, if they are adult enough to know right from wrong, and kindness from cruelty. You must answer this question yourself. If you dislike the attitude and personality of people who act as if they do not care about others, and how it makes you feel when it is aimed directly at you, do you wish to become one of them? This is the question you are asking after all.

If you choose to join them I just want you to know that should we ever meet, should you decide to show me how little you care about me, it will not alter the fact that I will likely care even more about you when we part. I will be feeling sad for all the joy you will miss or push away from your life because you did not care. I will never care about your opinion of me, but I will always care about you, your health, and wellbeing. There is enough sadness without creating our own deliberately.

Good luck my friend. You walk your path alone your entire life, as it is unique to you. Try to become the kind of person you would enjoy walking with and keeping you company on your journey.

I hope I provide at least a single grain of a thought worth contemplating.

"Be picky about who you spend your time with lost time is worse than lost money!"

Be your strongest self

There are many ways to achieve greatness. Not one of them is easy. For no one. But there is a truth for all of us. It will pay off. No one is you and that is your superpower. Surround yourself with people who push you to be your best self.

You are your own ally in becoming your strongest self. Notice your immediate, "default" reactions- your most frequent thoughts, feelings, and impulsive reactions to stress and pressure. Take a few days to identify which reactive habits you need to update to fit your current vision, abilities, values, and challenges.

Remember how you felt when you helped a friend cope with a stressful or heart-breaking event? You observed their problem from a distance and shifted to the role of a compassionate, wise friend. Do this for yourself and experience the power of calmly observing old habits and thoughts from your larger, strongest self without identifying with them. Recall the feeling of playing in the zone at levels far beyond what your ego knows how to achieve. Play and work consistently in the zone by connecting your struggling limited sense of self with the rest of your brain and body. Only work with all parts of yourself integrated into the grander whole that is your strongest self.

Notice how "have to's" and self-criticism lead to stress and anxiety. Replace all self-threats with a message that makes you feel safe with you. Tell yourself: "Regardless of what happens, I will not make myself feel bad. I will not let any event or person determine my worth."

Label your stress levels on a scale of one to ten (where "one" means safety and "ten" is the worse stress ever).

Within one to two weeks, your body will quickly calm down when you say, for example, "It's only a three. We won't die. I can live with this. It's safe to stop the stress response."

Consider that many forms of shame and depression may be ancient (mammal brain) survival mechanisms to keep us from fighting in situations where we cannot win and to maintain social structure, such as bowing to those in power. Use your new human brain to maintain your worth, consider your higher values, and override any lower brain archaic reactions that no longer fit. Use the symptoms of procrastination, ambivalence, or indecision, the inner conflict between two primitive parts, "You have to" versus "I don't want to" to evoke your new human brain's unique ability to choose what to do and to take responsibility for the consequences.

Change "I don't know" to "I wonder what will come to me." Watch for the surprise as the creative side of your brain starts working to bring you from "not knowing" to "knowing."

Self-Love

"If you don't see your own value, you'll choose to have people around you who don't see it either."

Everything you are going through is because God is preparing you for what you asked for

I know a woman who tells me that she is waiting for God to send her the man of her life, but she was dating a married man. I ask, "How do you think God is going to put the man of your life in front of you if you are dating this married man? How exactly do you think this works?" Moving forward, this odd couple went out to eat at the same restaurant, sitting in the same table for a little over two years. They also always had the same waiter which kept their table saved for them every time. They saw each other every week. One day she asks me, "Diosa why do you tell me that God is not going to send me the right man?" I respond, "I'm going to tell you something that my mother taught me. (Long ago I tell my mother, "Mom, I want a new car and I'm praying to God and working hard so that I can buy it." Meanwhile, there was an older vehicle that my parents had gifted me already taking space in the driveway. Therefore, she responds to my news like this... "Ok Joanne, but don't forget that the other car is parked outside." I respond, "Ok mom." Every time I got paid, I would tell my mother I was a step closer to getting the car I wanted. All she kept repeating was, "ok my daughter, but don't forget that the other car is there." A couple of weeks have passed and again I tell my mother that in days I will have my car. What do you think she responded? "Ok Joanne, but don't forget that the car is there." I ask myself, why does mom always tell me the same thing about the other car? I stopped to think and asked her, "Mom, why is it that every time I try to tell you something positive about the car that I want, you tell me something about the old car?" She responds with a question. 'Look my daughter if you buy the new car where are you going to put it?" I started thinking and said that I understood. I took the keys of the old car and took it to a buy here pay here dealer where they buy used cars and luckily for me the car that I wanted to buy elsewhere was also being sold at the same dealer. I was going to pay double for the car that I wanted at the other dealer. When I took the old car, they accepted it as a form of payment and not only did I pay less, I was also able to return home with my new car. Something so unplanned. I thought I was not ready financially to obtain the vehicle I wanted yet, but God is good. I get home and show my mom my new car, and she says; "of course, you got your new car honey. But it only happened because you got rid of the old car.")

Getting to the point of the conversation I was having with this lovely woman I say, "So you see, you cannot ask God for anything if you are not ready to receive it." As I speak to her she starts crying and says, "oh my God. You are right, I am not ready to receive." Well, in time she left the married man. One day this woman goes to a store where coincidentally bumps into the waiter who use to serve her when she was with the married man. He sees her and says, "Hello. I haven't seen you guys around in a long time." She responds, "I am no longer with him." The waiter replies excited, "finally! I was waiting more than two years for this to happen. I never understood why you were with him because he would take his wife there too." Moving forward, as another year or so pass, this woman is now married to that waiter with children. As of today, he is no longer a waiter but the owner of three restaurants. She is an investment banker which coincidentally was the piece he was missing. Today they are both business owners and live a beautiful life. You know why? She returned the old car.

If you also have an old car, but you are asking for a new one, make sure you make the space for it. God is waiting for you to make the space to send you what you desire. That could be the situation in your relationship or with anything else you want in life. If I were you, I would try.

"Being good is easy, the hard part is being fair."

Psychological (Emotional) abuse is worse than physical abuse

The scars of emotional abuse are very real, and they run deep. You may think that physical abuse is far worse than emotional abuse since physical violence can send you to the hospital and leave you with physical wounds. Emotional abuse can be just as damaging—sometimes even more so. Abuse, both emotional and physical, leaves marks of trauma that haunts the person years after the abuse ends. When these people are asked to differentiate between the two to find out which has left the worse effect and needs treatment first, they differ in opinion mostly. Some are of the opinion that physical abuse traumatized their lives the most, while others are more haunted by the reminiscences of emotional abuse, they had faced any time in their lives.

Domestic violence, for example, can easily be fought against if women try to seek help from police and others that are more than willing to help victimized women. But a woman undergoing emotional abuse would not be able to do the same because of fear of being left when asked for witnesses and evidence. Abuse of any kind is a bad thing that should be condemned from happening. Women, men, and even kids must not tolerate any kind of abuse. At the same time people must learn to be patient and compassionate to their children who would unknowingly be subjected to emotional abuse if parents do not pay heed to their own behavior.

There is a big myth in our society that only women are subjected to abuse. Men are subjected to emotional and physical abuse too. Irrespective of gender and age, we must not tolerate abuse because being patient and waiting for it to stop on its own is the biggest mistake people make. Speak for yourself and for those around you who you suspect could be getting abused in any way. We are doing a better job picking up neglect and we are improving terms of recognizing some of the more subtle forms of trauma. But we still have a way to go in terms of emotional abuse and emotional neglect.

"Silent mistreatment, which is not accompanied by beatings, but silence, looks, reproaches... sinks you into the deepest, cancels you out, humiliates you, and worst of all, no one notices."

Push yourself today

People that do daring things, people who made history, people that have changed the cause of history. People that are making the dramatic difference on the planet. If you ask them what would make you face this kind of heat, this kind of fire, this kind of rejection. If you ask them, they will tell you, "It's worth it for me to do it". They found their pulse. They found their place. They found something inside themselves that has given them the strength to face the heat. While other people have become cowards and run away. They say I cannot do that. But others will stand forward and say I will, I will do it.

You must have that in you. You have the capability to make that happen in your life. Your life is worth whatever effort you are willing to put forward. You must be willing to reject the desire to be average. I do not want to be average. I want to be different. What is it that we find that will give us that tenacity? That will give us that courage to stand up. That will give us the kind of dedication and determination to come back again and again?
What would do that for us? How do you find that stuff?

It is worth it when you love it. Love will help you bridge a lot of challenges. It will help you handle many obstacles. You cannot let anyone take your freedom. If you finally found what you want or what suits you, say, "I want to do this!" You might catch a lot of heat for it but its ok, it is alright. Be willing to do that. That will drive you. It will keep you going.

Folks will look at you in total amazement saying, "How can she do that? Where does the energy come from?" I can tell you based upon my own experience that when you get going, when you can start coming at it again and again, you will not need anyone. Not anyone trying to take your freedom. Time will not let you stay young. "We don't care what they say, we're going to love who we want to love."

"Your future depends on you doing it today, not tomorrow."

What is the one thing holding you back from achieving what you want in life?

Weather its fear of failure. Fear of rejection. Fear of being alone, or fear of being hurt. All fears hold us back from what we are truly capable of. Fear of failure will prevent you from realizing your full potential. Fear of rejection will prevent you from meeting the love of your life. Fear of being alone will prevent you from ever truly knowing yourself. Fear of getting hurt will prevent you from experiencing some of life's richest beauties.

You can overcome any fear. The fastest way to deal with fear is to face it and move forward anyway. I have learned that the most successful people on this planet leverage the fear. They do not pretend it is not there and they do not fight with it either. They use fear. Fear can awaken you to your deepest possibilities when you learn to use it to your advantage.

You can make a habit of doing just that. The ability to overcome fear is a muscle you can build. You decide that you run your life and you will not be at the mercy of fear. Learn how I learned to overcome fear by taking massive actions. You will see how you can do it too. When you train yourself to face your fears you discover a level of freedom most people will never know. Join me and give it a try. You got this!

"The biggest communication problem is that we don't listen to understand."

Manifest who you are, and the Universe will align with you

It is important to manifest who you are in life. You need to be positive for yourself and for others weather we are around or not. Thinking something that is not positive or that shows you hold a type of grudge, even if it is a small one, will block your own blessings.

Stay happy. Stay focused and positive. Even if you are in an uncomfortable situation. If you have done nothing wrong or negative, you should not drain yourself about anything. Life always comes around and makes you see the full circle. If something negative happens to you it is because that is what you are attracting in your mind. It is not because of anyone else. No one has power over you but you.

Many of you have probably heard of The Law of Attraction. According to this belief system, our thoughts (both conscious and unconscious) dictate the reality of our lives. In essence, if you honestly believe that it is possible to have something you really want, you will create the reality of it in your life. What people often do not realize is that your attention and thoughts can also attract what you do not want.

All thoughts create a feeling. Feelings create the energy that forms the "magnet" that attracts what comes into our lives. For manifestation purposes it is particularly important to be aware of your thoughts, both positive and negative.

Fear and worry are immensely powerful feelings. If we allow thoughts that create fear and worry within us, that is exactly what we will draw into our lives – unease. When you have unease within, you are not aligned with the positive things you wish to attract. For instance, perhaps you want to manifest a new car into your life. You send out thoughts and feelings that set your intention for a new vehicle. Soon you start to worry. You ruminate on what could go wrong. "What if I get a new car, then get laid off tomorrow and can't pay for it?" Worrying about the "what ifs" puts you out of alignment with your intention. It is as though you have sent a mixed message to the Universe and now the Universe has no idea what you genuinely want.

Aligning yourself perfectly with your intentions is the key to manifestation. By being aware of your thoughts, you can indeed master this alignment process. It is a matter of paying attention to where your thoughts flow, and the feelings those thoughts create within you. When you are feeling upset or uneasy, trace back the thoughts that are creating this unease. Once you can pinpoint those thoughts, make a conscious effort to change or turn them around. One approach is to first imagine living the intention. Take a short trip into your mind and imagine that you already have what it is you want manifested into your life. How does having what you want make you feel? If any mixed emotions, fears or second thoughts are being evoked, then you need to adjust what it is you want to attract. Keep doing this until the object of your desire creates only positive feelings.

Let's say you set your intentions on a brand-new Mercedes-Benz SLR roadster with a sticker price of $495,000. Imagine that you own it. Are you worry-free and happy with it? Or do you worry about getting a scratch or ding each time you drive it? Does the thought of that monthly car payment make you feel sick in the pit of your stomach? These feelings are exactly what will tell the Universe, "No! I don't really want this in my life." Perhaps you should lower the price range of your desire and choose a car that is in the $30,000 range. See how that feels. If you experience feelings of ease within, then you are learning to align yourself with your intention. You are giving the Universe a crisp, clear signal of exactly what you want.

Remember that the key is to create the alignment by having only positive feelings attached to what it is you are manifesting. It may take a few times tweaking or changing your intentions. But once you have that total alignment, hold on tight – the Universe has a way of working very quickly!

~ *"Everything is energy… Match the frequency of the reality you want, and you can't help but get that reality. It can be no other way. This is not Philosophy. This is Physics."*

– Albert Einstein

There are no rules

Growing up I was bullied many times. I was made fun off because I was extremely tall for my age and very overweight. I had low self-esteem and never had a boyfriend. Not even friends in school. My oldest sister knew I did not have many friends, so her friends became my friends. That was good enough for me.

For many years I hated myself. I grew up acting like I never understood anything in life. Which led my family to think that I was not the brightest out of the bunch. I downgraded myself and even started to hurt myself at some point. My family never even knew. I would steal money from my parents to buy cookies and goodies at school. I would do so to give to kids, so they would be my friends. Yeah, I bought my friends. I even bought a boyfriend too! In middle school, some girl I did not even know, chose to fight me. Only because I had an extremely popular sister.

Throughout the years, I have been disliked and criticized by so many women that I do not even know. They dislike my features or the way I laugh. I can continue talking about the tragedies and obstacles I had to overcome but that is not what is important. All these unexpected events not only helped me become the daring woman I am today but also reminded me that I am vulnerable. In life there is no real safety except self believe.

With everything that happens daily in life, I started thinking that life has no rules. And I was correct. There are no rules if you are a man. If you are a woman, you must play the game. What is the game? You are allowed to be pretty. You are allowed to be cute, sexy. Don't act too smart. Don't have an opinion that is out of line with the status. You are allowed to be objective. Dress like a slut but do not own your sluttiness. Do not share your own sexual fantasies with the world. Noooo! Be what men want you to be. Most importantly feel comfortable with you being around other men. Finally, do not age because to age is a sin. You will be criticized. You will be downgraded. At that aging point of your life you are worth nothing. That is the game. Is that even believable?

As women we must start appreciating our own worth and each other's worth. Seek out a strong woman to befriend. To align yourself with. To learn from. To be inspired by. To collaborate with, to support, to be enlightened by-instead of criticizing each other and slandering ourselves for pleasure. Sometimes we take grudges for love. We admire ourselves so much that instead of giving a compliment, we say, "look at that girl, she thinks she's all that". But that's not the idea. Let us stand together instead of bringing each other down. I assure you we will have more success pulling each other up.

"When you have exhausted all possibilities, remember this; you have not."

If you say you are leaving

If you won't love me, don't write to me. If you're not staying, don't look for me. If you're not going to be with me, don't seduce me. If you say you're leaving, don't come back.

I have tried thousands of times to hold you back so that you remember or notice what we could have been. I know I will survive. I do not have anything else to give because I gave it to you and even that still was not enough. I hope you find what you are looking for if you know what that is. If you come back, I am warning you that if you say that you are leaving, the door will be open. Once you leave it will close. Not for a while, forever.

The only thing that hurts is the time wasted on a person who does not exist. Do not worry because I will get used to living without you. I always did because you were never there. Take your hypocrisies and fake kisses, because as Borges said, "I have learned that kisses are not contracts and gifts are not promises".

I do know that you can plant your own garden and decorate your own soul instead of waiting for someone to bring you flowers. I got tired of your lies and everything has an expiration date. I will step over the past and be present for the present.

Remember if you say it's over or if you say you're leaving, please please please, don't come back. You left? I loved you. Goodbye

"Do not open your mouth if you're not going to be doing what you're feeling."

The three things I learned while my plane crashed (Ric Elias Story)

I would like to tell you a story that moved me and changed my life. After listening to it I was no longer the same. The story is about this man named Ric Elias, maybe you have heard of it or not. This man gave a speech on Ted Talks, and for those who don't know, Ted Talks is a wonderful place where the best wisdom of the whole world reunites. With a three-minute talk this man changed the life of all the people who were there. I am going to repeat a bit of what he said and maybe in three minutes a lot of us will no longer think or be the same. The title of his talk that is completely real, "The three things I learned while my plane crashed." Ric Elias was on a plane with two hundred passengers. Suddenly the plane made a strange maneuver. Ric asks the stewardess, "hey did something happen?" She responds, "No don't worry, those movements happen naturally." But the plane had lost an engine! However, right after the plane made another noise. Now they had lost the second engine. Right when Ric was about to ask the stewardess again, the pilot says on the audio system... "Prepare for impact!" Ric, logically asked himself, "Well I no longer have a need to ask do I?"

He knew that he was going to die. Ric says that at that time he thought three things. The first, that everything changes in an instant. We don't realize it, but it is true. He then thought of everything he did not do. In all the people he wanted to reach out to and didn't. In all the fences he wanted to bend, and all the risks he should have taken, yet didn't. Ric says in that talk that from that moment he learned that he never wants to put off anything in life. He says that he no longer has good wine in his winery, that he has drank it all. He came up with a phrase that says, "I collect bad wine" whatever old wine you have that you want to save he will take it, and he will be drinking it. With that message he does not mean to get drunk tonight and finish everything you have in one night. He means that every minute of life is to be enjoyed because this is real. We always live with our backs turned to death and we never want to know anything about it. Every minute can be the last.

The second thing Rick thought when the plane was crashing, was in the amount of time he had lost because of his ego. On the amount of time he had wasted on things that do not matter with people who do matter.
Rick says that since that moment he has not argued with his wife again. That between being right and being happy, he chooses to be happy. The third thing he learned is that death is not scary. I think that most of us think that dying is scary, but he says that dying is not scary, and the plane was crashing. He said, "It's as if all our lives we were preparing for death." Ric stated, "Dying is not scary, but you feel very sad because you love life."

That day Ric survived; he was one of the passengers on the plane that fell into the Hudson River. Nevertheless, I must point out that it was indeed a very heroic Pilot who drove the plane and managed to save the lives of most people. Ric ends the talk by saying that all of us are flying today, and we do not know if our plane is going to crash tonight. I loved the last words from the three-minute talk that say, "You're not going to live forever. Ask yourself only one thing. Are you being the best person you can be?" Are you?

This human being is a great example of life and life is now.

"You should not be afraid of death, but of never beginning to live."

A dreamer

Advancing years ago, the only people on earth were monkeys. And they said, "We'll never walk erectus. We'll never use tools. We'll never talk". And then one monkey said, "oh yeah? Well, I'm talking right now". That monkey was a dreamer.

Fast forward 500 years. The Wright brothers decide to make themselves a flying machine. "You fool. You idiots". "What's your problem?" everyone shouted! "That will never work because plywood weighs more than air" To which the Wright brothers responded, "no it doesn't" The Wright brothers were dreamers.

The Earls of sandwich and Sir Francis Bacon. Had it not been for them, the BLT would merely be lettuce and tomato. They were dreamers, and sandwich makers.

Vincent van Gogh. Everyone told him, "you only have one ear, you cannot be a great artist". And you know what he said? "I can't hear you". Vincent Van Gogh was a dreamer.

Louis Pasteur turned cheese into medicine. Genius dreamer!

Benjamin Franklin, people said, "you can't fly a kite in a rainstorm", and Ben Franklin said, "Yes you can, if you have an electric kite". He was an awesome dreamer.

A man who broke more bones than any man in history, Evel Knievel. A definite dreamer.

Joanne Suarez known as Diosa. She was told by knowledgeable and experienced Doctors that after having a second stroke there was a seventy five percent chance that she would not walk actively again. Nor regain full strength of the area affected by the stroke. Diosa said, "oh really? I might not regain full strength, but I will walk and even run actively beside my children again". Diosa is also a great dreamer!

As an Afro Cuban American woman, I must say that I am so proud of who I am and where my roots and ancestors come from. The movie Black Panther was a big deal for me, my kids, friends, and the entire world. I would like to thank Chadwick Boseman for showing that there are many avenues for us. Your role gave us hope and confidence. A man who fought colon cancer for four years and still strived to make and leave a great legacy. He had a dream. "It was the honor of his career to bring King T'Challa to life in Black Panther". Chadwick Boseman was a dreamer, believer, and a leader. Wakanda Forever!

Photo courtesy of ABC12 ksat.com

Dare to dream. Dream your wildest dreams. You can climb the highest mountain, or you can drown in a teacup. (If you find a big enough teacup). But if somebody tells you that you cannot do something you say, "Yes I can!" Because I am doing it right now.

"Not everyone can become a great Artist, but a great Artist can come from anywhere!"

Pandemic

Around the world, people are reflecting. Around the world, people are looking at their neighbors in a different way. Around the world, people are waking up to a new reality. We are waking up to the reality of how big we really are to have the little control we hold. Today we think about what really matters. In giving Love. In being loved. Let us pray and remember:

Yes, there is fear, but there does not have to be hatred.

Yes, there is isolation, but there does not have to be loneliness.

Yes, there is panic shopping, but it does not have to be bad.

There are also lots of deaths, but there can always be a rebirth of love. There is also passion for what we do in life and we are the example of that. In our union we have strength. Life is now. The only thing that can work against the pandemic we are presently living is self-love and our union in peace and harmony. Let's work together. Regardless, it is up to us to get better. Think about that positively.

"The fact that humanity has to clarify that any life matters should be a cause for concern!"

It's not Love

What does love mean to you? Why do I have people asking me what love is? Or do you think this person loves me? If you ever have to wonder if the person you are with loves you, that is not love. I am not trying to create any kind of separation between anyone, but I speak reality.

If you are asking if this person loves you or not, most likely no. To me it is not love. Love begins with loving yourself. I have a friend who called me to ask me, "Do you think my husband loves me"? I tell her "I don't know", and she tells me: "I'm so used to abuse that I think that's what love is". I said, "No, you are not used to abuse. What really happened is that you never learned to love yourself. When you learn to love yourself, you will understand what love is".

That is why you must set the tone of your life. When you do that your life will accept nothing less, period. Many of us have accepted someone else's definition of love and we believe that is what love is. We believe that love is enough. True? "He gives me enough". But love goes beyond friendship and relationships too. We settle for the minimum. Someone who really cares about you is not going to want to put questions in your life. The one who really loves you tells you how it is. I do not want to create doubts or ask questions in my partner's life. I never want you to wonder if I want it. On the contrary, I want you to know it above, and in abundance. I want my children to know how much I care.

Why is it the same? It's as if your kids wonder, "Does mommy love me?" "Does daddy love me?" That should not be a question. They should know. When it comes to your life, make sure you give that 110% to the person you are with. Make sure you do your best. They should never question you. They should never question your loyalty. They should never ask if you appreciate them, they should know all these things. Many of us know what it is. We just refuse to believe it for whatever reason. It could be so much for fear of being alone or the fear of depending only on ourselves. Just have common sense. These are just facts and maybe you need to hear it from someone else. But you know what it is. If not, you would not ask yourself the question repeatedly. Someone who really loves you, leaves you no doubt. They leave you certainty.

"One of the hardest things you'll have to do is mourn the loss of a person who is still alive."

Your healing is your responsibility

Many of you depend on the person who has hurt you to heal you. We wonder why we endure the pain. It is not their responsibility to heal you. Healing is your responsibility.

Stop waiting for an apology to heal you -- Stop waiting for the person who hurt you to heal you -- Stop waiting for the closure to heal -- Stop waiting for understanding or plain anything to heal you --Stop empowering someone else to heal you when it is your responsibility, not theirs -- Stop waiting for these things to heal you and start your healing journey.

Yes, the healing journey sucks. To be real with you it is hard, and it is not fun. It is a process. You are going to have your ups and downs. But you cannot wait for that person to give you something when what they first gave you was pain. They are the reason why you are healing to begin with.

Do not put your heart in the hands of who broke it anymore. These are just facts. What I need you to do is take responsibility for your life. Take responsibility for being a better you. Take responsibility for your progress. Take ownership of your life because if you don't, you will be controlled by someone else. You will end up accepting the definition of love from someone who does not love you. Do you know what you are accepting? A lesser version of yourself until you look in the mirror and do not even realize who you are. You become the pain they gave you. This is a reminder of who you are.

"One man's desert is another man's theme park. I choose my friends for their good looks, my acquaintances for their good character, and my enemies for their good intellect."

Get your priorities straight

We all go through different phases in our lives, and some of those phases have transitional periods where our day-to-day lives can be a bit more confusing than normal. Sometimes these phases get dragged out, or we do not even know why we are in them to begin with. Suddenly we look around and we are not quite on the path we meant to be on. When you do not have your priorities in order, it is easy to go off the rails. And while it is certainly possible to get back on track, you first must be aware of the problem. Here is how to tell if you need to get your priorities straight so you can move on with your life. When you think about how you want to live your life, what exactly comes to mind? Do you see yourself traveling the world, writing a book, or building your own business? However, you choose to live your life will most likely be determined by how you set your priorities. When you want to make changes to your life, it is important to know what is most valuable to you. Though it can be hard to figure this out when you are always in the fast lane and you start to lose focus on what you originally wanted in the first place.

We all live such busy lives these days and it makes it challenging to do everything on our to-do list. To make sure you can focus on your priorities it is important you ask yourself the 'why' behind everything you do. Once you have a deeper understanding of why something is important to you, it makes it easier to follow through with getting it done. You may even find once you discover your 'why' that sometimes your priorities will even shift.

So how do you figure out what is most important so you can set your priorities straight? It begins with you. It starts with you. You must commit to making time for yourself. Getting caught up in the details of life can cloud your vision around what is most important to you. Even taking short amounts of time to breath, relax, process and plan will help you reduce the clutter and see more clearly what you may have been missing before.

People often get confused with priorities to the point they do not notice they have been spending too much money on the wrong things. For example, at times some people have had the need to buy certain things extremely necessary for their home but it is postponed because they pretend to find that having a happy moment and feeling good for the time being is what is more important. Some of us even say "life is short, we only have one life to live" so, they feel that should be their priority. That could be a fact "life may be short" but we should not walk around life with that in mind because it is also part of the law of attraction. Repeating "life is short" too often can lead to your reality. At some point in the future you may find yourself stuck in a situation where you need this one important thing you chose not to buy over having fun, and thinking life is short. You even ask yourself... "Where did I go wrong?"

If you want to get a clear picture of where you want your life to head, here are ten ways you can figure out how you want to take charge of your life by setting your priorities straight.

1. Figure out what's most important to you

Before you can set your priorities, you need to figure out exactly what they are. How do you expect to kill it when you have no idea what your goals are? You have limited time and energy, so you need to determine what your top two priorities are at any given moment. For instance, one may be to get a new job and the other may be look for a new apartment. These are both quite hefty tasks requiring laser tight focus, so my suggestion in this scenario is to look for a job first. Once you land it, then you can narrow your apartment search to somewhere nearby your new office.

2. Create a plan

It's time to put your thoughts into action. Take a few moments to create a plan of where you would like to see yourself in the next couple of months or years. Align those dreams with your priorities to help you focus on making your wishes come true. Jot down what you are looking for in a new job, get specific in terms of salary, location, and the type of role as well as where your strengths are. Also, what you want to learn and expand upon in the next twelve months. Then create an action plan. Set up job alerts. Revise your resume. Network with two people each week, etc.

3. Determine how you want to live your life

Another great way to keep your priorities straight is to consider how you want to live your life. If you want to work only a certain number of hours per week, but your current job prevents you from doing that, then finding a new job might take precedent on your to-do list. It is important to have your priorities straight, so you are living a life of purpose and fulfillment that feels good for you. When you have your priorities straight and know what is important to you, you are more in line with your intentions and what you really want out of life.

4. Talk to a mentor

Talking to a mentor can open your eyes to problems you may not have never noticed. They might help you see things from a different perspective and challenge you to focus on what needs to be number one in your life. If you are not sure what is most important, talk to a mentor as well as friends. They may be able to help you not only in terms of practicality, but also judge the sense of urgency and emotion in your voice. If you constantly complain about your job and dread going into the office every day, they will instantly know you should put that at the top of your list of priorities.

5. Eliminate distractions

If you want to set your priorities straight, you need to get rid of the distractions. Turn off the TV and throw your phone out the window, it is time to focus on bettering your life and leaving the clutter out the door. Set aside time on your calendar to set your priorities. For me, I realized I click on every article that pops up in my Facebook feed. I must reduce doing that. These kinds of distractions take up more time during the day and create more interruptions than we realize. Start calling yourself out on things like that so you can clear out the clutter. Set a timer on social media if you must as well. You will be surprised how much hidden time you discover to focus on pursuing your priorities.

6. Take time to reflect

This means setting aside an afternoon or a block of time where you shut off your phone, put pen to paper and tell yourself that, even though you have a million things going on, this is a priority. For instance, let's say you work in a toxic environment and you have not gotten a raise in two years. Hello, job search!! Analyze your life and figure out what kind of changes you need to make. If you feel like you have no time to do this, then honestly, that is even more of a reason for you to reflect.

7. Be honest with yourself

You must check those priorities with reality. Keep track of how much time you truly spend on things each week, for at least a week or maybe two. Be honest. Finally, compare the reality of your time with your ideal priorities. Are you giving proper time to what matters most to you? If not, why not? What can you do to make your true priorities number one in your life? Make appropriate changes so your reality matches what really matters most to you. I am sorry to say, but sometimes you need to get hit with a healthy dose of reality to realize what you truly need. While you do not want to place a lot of pressure on yourself, you do need to be honest with yourself to figure out what is most important.

8. Remember that it is normal for your priorities to change

As you get older, your priorities will most likely change. Do not think of it as a bad thing. Consider the fact that over time you mature, and you need to just reprioritize what is most important. First, we must have awareness around the fact that our priorities will change as our lives and circumstances change. Some priorities will be ones that we focus on over the long term and other priorities will be focused on what is happening right now. I recommend that you make two lists: Main and active areas of your life and secondary areas or areas that do not need as much attention currently. Spend some time to go over each area of your life and write out any ideas or priorities that will be helpful to incorporate into your life now or in the future.

9. Create a list

For myself, there is nothing more satisfying than creating a list. It is a great way to see what I truly value so I can figure out what my next step needs to be. When we feel overwhelmed it can be challenging to figure out what our priorities are because everything can feel equally as important. A great tip to keep your priorities straight is to make a list of everything weighing on your mind. Just get it all out on paper. Once you see it in front of you, it already starts to feel more manageable. From there, rate each item on a scale from one to ten based on importance. By doing this you will be able to determine which priorities should come first.

10. Check in with yourself regularly

When you figure out what your priorities are, check in with yourself to make sure you stay focused and conquer them. Schedule a coffee date with yourself in your calendar so you do not forget. Check in regularly with yourself, often! Ask if your priorities are still serving you? Are you holding yourself accountable to living your life on your terms? Do not get frustrated if you need some time to figure out what your priorities are so you can set them straight. Be kind to yourself and remember that it is completely normal for your priorities to change over time. Eventually, with a little bit of patience (and a lot of wine), you can figure out what is most important and take charge of your life.

"Disappointments reposition priorities... I thank them from time to time."

Self-love is the cure for self-hate

Do you love yourself? How much? If you understand the value of self-love, you will be wise to whom you have in your circle. Most people out here are living empty. They have no sense of self. No sense of self love. When I say self-love, it has nothing to do with money, materialistic things, or any of the other things your negative mind can possibly think of. It has nothing to do with appearance. It has nothing to do with what you drive or any of those superficial things that one would assume can make you love yourself even more. It is a matter of knowing your value. It is a matter of knowing you do not have to be around those people in those types of environments or situations for you to finally see the value in yourself.

I love me independent of you loving me.
I believe in me.
I know myself worth.
I know clearly that I'm a child of God and God has a purpose over my life and if he didn't, I wouldn't be here right now.
I am here, and I have a purpose.

There is no value in having wisdom, knowledge, inside spirituality if there is no love. Every day I am a work in progress. Self-love is the cure to self-hate.

I don't like you. I don't trust you. I know you're talking shit about me from behind my back.

Why would anybody who genuinely loves themselves hang out with or mess with those type of people? Now, here are the worst type of people in the world in my book. The people who literally hate your guts and dislike you in every way and you don't have a clue they feel this way about you because they're able to cover up all of their malicious energy and intentions towards you without giving you no trace that they dislike you. You had no clue but then you finally find out, and you are stun!

When people show you who they are, and you see it to the point that you're able to talk about it. "Can you believe what she said about me?" Now you know and you were able to talk about it. Then again you get an invite from the same person who hurt you which in fact were just sitting over a minute crying about and yet, you agree to show up. Really? Love yourself so that you can stop hanging out with these types of people. Nobody who loves themselves will ever entertain the idea of being around these types of people. Love yourself. You work too hard to hang out with somebody that just wants to talk about how you can make easy money. Men up and say "So guess what homie, go get your money. Go do whatever you have to do to double or triple your money. I'm out of here because I don't want to be on the receiving end of whatever those consequences are that may come from your wrongdoing". I know you all know many of those type of people. Doing a lot of negative, crazy, and dysfunctional shit every single day.

Then you have these special women that you also don't need in your circle. There's this one that calls herself your friend but is always jealous and envious of others. She talks negative about every girl she sees to you and talk about everything they're doing. Who they date? Who they are sleeping with? So, my question is... You don't think she is also talking about you? Are you that special to where your homegirl talks shit about everybody, and you don't think she is talking about you? So, when people show you who they are, you must believe it, and you must make the adjustment according to all these things that are revealed to you.

Now your family is mean, evil, and spiteful, condescending and messed up but you're desperate for the validation. "That's my family you know!" That is what most of us say. "I know they can be mean talking about me and my kids, but you know, that's family, right? That's family!" Oooh so, they can tear you down because they are family? Dealing with them hurts even deeper because we have the same blood in our bloodstream. I rather a random person in the street talk downgrading things about me and tear me down versus my own family.

I love me.
I see the value in me.
I must be careful of who and what I give emotional access to.

My children have given me a bottom line. My children have created a new standard for me. My kids have changed my life forever. I did not know what love was until we met. What does that mean? It means you will never see me at dinner. You will never see me hanging out or doing just anything with anybody. I do not care who you are or how much money you are worth. I have visions, I have ideas and I have goals. Now, I believe in connecting with people on a human level, but I am on a mission and goal oriented.
That is who I am!

You cannot get to the next level with all the devils that you have in your life. You have so many negative, mean, evil, malicious, and dysfunctional people in your life and around your circle. This is the reason why you cannot clear out the clutter and get to the next level. Self-love is the cure to self-hate!

I will repeat it again self-love is the cure to self-hate!

And I began to get rid of everything that was not healthy, situations, people, friends, family, and just things. They called it selfishness, I called it self-love.
-Therapy in Sessions

Speak your truth

Have you ever been talking about someone and your phone butt dials the person you are talking about? I have learned that thanks to that now this person knows how I feel, and we are in a better place. We must learn to speak up and say what you feel no matter how hurtful it may be. Do not live in a fake reality. Speaking your truth comes from knowing who you are, from self-knowledge, and knowing your purpose in life.

Your purpose is something you do. It is something you are called to become. As with many things in life, achieving your purpose can sometimes take a lifetime of practice. "Living with integrity means: Not settling for less than what you know you deserve in your relationships. Asking for what you want and need from others. Speaking your truth, even though it might create conflict or tension. Behaving in ways that are in harmony with your personal values. Making choices based on what you believe, and not what others believe."

At some point in your life you made the decision that it was no longer safe to speak your truth. In your early years, speaking up led to a scolding from your parents, or worse. Their censure caused pain and engendered a belief in you that speaking up would create even more pain. This belief compelled you to withhold and question your voice from then on. Your parents, of course, did the best they could give their challenging upbringing; but whether they knew it or not, they were recreating their painful past where they were to be seen but not heard, and forced to cope with their difficulties and feelings by keeping a tight lip.

The cycle repeated itself in how they raised you, and in how they expected you to keep certain parts of yourself invisible. Even if your parents were generally kind and open to you, so long as they held onto their need to withdraw-their coping strategies-they would unintentionally invite you to withdraw as well; you would likely inherit their fears, beliefs and attitudes, like the innocent sponge and mimicker you were. Withdrawing serves a purpose: to protect ourselves from being hurt.

If we play by house rules, and not rock the boat with "endless" questions, "irrational" imaginations and "childish antics", we are safe. But the need to withdraw in childhood perpetuates into our teen and adult years when we continue believing we need to protect ourselves. The childhood belief crystalizes into an attitude and behavioral pattern that engrain into our psyche and lives. The belief is identified, and we go from needing to withdraw as a child, to being withdrawn as a teen and adult. Afraid of our voice and fearful of getting hurt, so we choose not to speak our truth.

Speak your truth even if your voice shakes.

~ *"I'm not rude, I just say what everyone else is thinking"*

How to be happy everyday (Give a Smile challenge)

I have what some consider one of the toughest jobs on the planet. I am a Mother! Yesssss!!! I am the mother of two terribly busy children who magically think that I am a doctor, baker, coach, chef, therapist, and that I have the patience of a saint twenty-four seven. I really do my best, and some days are definitely better than others. Especially in that part of having the patience of a saint. I want for my children what most parents want for their children. I want them to have a happy childhood. I want them to be free to play and make friends. May they grow up to be loving, compassionate, and happy adults but there seems to be a little challenge. The World Happiness Report states that at any given time, more than 220 million children and 1 billion adults suffer from anxiety, depression, and conduct disorders. Not exactly a pretty picture of happy people on a happy planet, is it? Unfortunately, as adults whether you are a parent or not, this is what our children are learning from us. They see how busy we are every day. They see our stress and they see us struggle to find our own happiness. So how do we go from anxiety and depression to being happy?

There is good news! The World Report on Happiness also states that the best indicator of whether a child becomes a satisfied adult is through their emotional health and childhood. So, if I have this right, it should be easy. Happy children, happy adults, happy planets, yeah?! Well, this is the exact same lesson that I learned from my career. When I was working in the hospital every Christmas morning we used to go with our patients and take them out of their rooms and sing and dance for them. If you could see the smile on their faces. We did this every Christmas morning for years, and those patients danced and sang with us. Their smiles would light up the hospital. This is what I have learned from our singing and dancing. Giving back to those patients made them happy, and it made me happy too! Now, we have heard that giving makes you happy and that giving is better than receiving, but have you really thought about why?

Well, researchers around the world have been studying the science and psychology of giving. They discovered that our brains and bodies are programmed to forgive. When we give our endorphins kick in, it gives us this natural feeling of euphoria. In fact, they have called it "the helpers high." Our oxytocin levels rise. "Note to those of you who have been searching for the fountain of youth, it is our body's natural anti-aging remedy! "That feeling I got when I sang and danced for these patients. That serotonin is our body's happy transmitter. But here's the icing on the cake, our cortisol levels go down. This is our stress hormone. Giving reduces. Anxiety and stress, and it makes us happy. Now, what if I told you that you can be happy every day and it's simple. In fact, it's so simple that a two-year-old can do it.

Since my son has a lot of tantrums and is always getting upset, I came up with a plan! I decided that I was going to teach him how he can be happy daily. I was now going to teach Nazier to give. I present the idea over cookies with ice cream. "Nazier, we are going to start this super fun family project together, we are going to give back to the world every day for a year!" Now, I waited to see the emotion on his face. That emotion he was feeling, and instead he says mommy, and how many days does a year have? Oh yeah, not exactly the answer I was looking for. On the other hand, Nazier is only seven years old, so I had to approach his daily idea of giving a little differently. So, little by little I began to explain to him and I said Nazier, we are going to do one thing to be kind, helpful, and generous to a person, an animal or the planet itself every day for 365 days.

Now when I share this idea with friends and family, they thought I was being a bit ambitious. I was going to give back to the world every day
for 365 days with a seven-year-old boy. So, I agreed that it seems like a lot, but not when you start small. My son and I started making a list of the different places we were going to go and the many things we were going to donate. Then he really noticed we were really going to do this and got excited! In fact, he even wanted to start the same day. Later in the week we set the day and went for it. We stopped at McDonald's, bought a bunch of burgers, and my son asked me. "Mom, is all this food for people the people who don't have money to buy it?" I respond yes; and you can immediately see how Nazier's little brain starts working. He was making that connection that his daily donation was going to help those people. Nazier learned that first day and turned to me, smiled, and said, "you are amazing mom, giving to those people has made me so happy!"

Daily donations quickly became routine for Nazier, just like brushing his teeth. Well now that I think about it, it would be easier to teach a seven-year-old to give every day than to brush his teeth every day. For sure! Well, what happens next? Nazier asked if we can share our daily giving adventures with our friends and family so they can be happy too. His idea came into play, and we have now started a blog. It's called: "give a smile challenge." So now we challenge you to participate in this unique kid-driven giving experience. They choose how they will give. Support the cause because they will impact the world in any way they choose.

This challenge was created for children, but it is for all of us. It doesn't matter where you live. What you are doing or how old you are! Imagine if we all did! For example, let's take about two thousand people for three hundred and sixty-five gifts a day. That's more than seven hundred thousand gifts a day. It is no longer just a child giving every day, but each one of us. Creating a better and happier world. It is so simple that a two-year-old can do it. It is a daily habit, like brushing your teeth.

Start your list today. Take a look at your life, your world, your family, your day, and do what works for you. Donate, volunteer, feed an animal, help a neighbor, and be nice to a stranger because that's how we're going to go from anxiety and depression to happiness. Together we can start small and make the world a better and happier place, one smile at a time.

"They told me I can choose anything. I chose to be happy."

Meaningful and memorable

With just a little effort, we can create powerful movements that last long in our souls and memories. We must fight for our life during those bad days to win the best days of our life. Let's make a difference. I challenge you to enter this unique donation experience. You choose how you are going to give and support the cause because you will impact the world in the way you choose.

Start your list today. You are going to do one thing to be kind, helpful, and generous. Be it for a person, an animal, or the planet itself at least one day of each week. For best results in a recurring happy attitude, I suggest you give daily. Take a look at your life, your world, your family, your day, and do what works for you. But please do it. (Thank me later)

Be part of this great adventure as it is the only way you can transform anxiety and depression into happiness. We can all start small and together create a healthier and happier world one day, one donation, one week, one month and one year at a time.

Share your experiences, videos, or images on my blog. Let's expand our vision together!

www.therapyinsessions.com

" To be meaningful, the service does not have to be large or ostentatious."

"A note to self...

You have been doubted, hated, talked about, made fun of, hurt, lied to, broken and at your wits end. With that being said, I commend you for the fact that you are still standing. Your courage speaks volumes! I know your struggles and the pain you've endured. You are more than a conqueror. Nothing can keep you down and no one can steel your joy. Don't you dare give up! Continue to stand tall and love yourself first. I believe in you!

You are appreciated,

Self"

"Get out of the rat race and take your career into your own hands."

Think outside the box!

Answer:

Here is the result. Congrats! You have connected 4 lines in a 9-dot pattern without lifting your pen or pencil or retracing any line. So, what are you pretending not to know? Did this exercise challenge your mind? Some of you did not get it and I'll tell you why. You have envisioned your life in a box. It is time to think outside the box. See where "outside the box" comes from?

There was no directive given about staying within a box, but our minds tend to build a box there, and a constraint is instantly put in place. Thinking outside the box is about dispensing with constraints-as many as possible. That's what the solution above does, and that's what the most effective kind of original and innovative thinking also does. If you aim at the same target everyone else is aiming at, your shots will end up where everyone else's do. If you till the same soil that everyone else tills, plant the same seeds they plant, and use the same water, you'll get the same garden. My point is that the minute you introduce a goal in your thinking, you're introducing a constraint. Your mind now has a direction, and it will tend to go in that direction.

Thinking outside the box simply means that you're willing to consider different solutions and methods for reaching your desired outcome. That is to say: You want to get from point A to Z, but you don't necessarily need or want to take the tried and true route to get there. Thinking differently can have a powerful and positive effect on your career. As an entrepreneur, here's why you need to think outside the box and how it can help you get ahead:

If everyone just accepted things the way they are, then there would never be any innovation or improvement in the world. If Thomas Edison had shrugged and figured things were good enough the way they were with gas lamps, light bulbs, and the electricity to power them might never have been developed. If he hadn't thought outside the box, the world could be a very dim (literally) place.

If you view things as unchangeable, then nothing will ever change for the better. By thinking outside the box and questioning the status quo, you'll constantly be considering how you could improve an experience, product, or service.

This allows you to keep growing-and can lead to intelligent and forward-thinking decisions in business.

Think outside the box as it will definitely give you a greater perspective. The world can become ridiculously small if you're close-minded. Thinking outside the box can expand your worldview, allowing you to have greater perspective on the events and happenings in your career (and in life). When you're willing to consider alternative points of view and ways of doing things, you'll be more open to a variety of different points of view and potential solutions.

A greater perspective can make you more receptive to different ideas, which means that you won't be limited by a small worldview. When you're open to limitless possibilities, the possibilities are endless! Think beyond. Expand your vision. Live life to the fullest. It all starts with you.

Peace and Love

~" But out of limitations comes creativity"
-Debbie Allen

EMBRACE WHO YOU ARE!

IT ALL STARTS WITH YOU

Peace & Love